BORROWED BIBLES

Also by Jim Good

Conrad Kriegbaum and His Creekpaum Descendants 2000

Robert Good and His Descendants 2000

Robert Good and His Descendants, Revised Edition 2011

BORROWED BIBLES

A MEMOIR

JIM GOOD

A DIVISION OF WRITER'S DIGEST

Borrowed Bibles
A Memoir

Copyright © 2012 Jim Good

Front cover courtesy of Brent C. Powell.

All rights reserved. No part of this book may be used or reproduced by any means, graphic, electronic, or mechanical, including photocopying, recording, taping or by any information storage retrieval system without the written permission of the publisher except in the case of brief quotations embodied in critical articles and reviews.

Abbott Press books may be ordered through booksellers or by contacting:

Abbott Press
1663 Liberty Drive
Bloomington, IN 47403
www.abbottpress.com
Phone: 1-866-697-5310

Because of the dynamic nature of the Internet, any web addresses or links contained in this book may have changed since publication and may no longer be valid. The views expressed in this work are solely those of the author and do not necessarily reflect the views of the publisher, and the publisher hereby disclaims any responsibility for them.

Any people depicted in stock imagery provided by Thinkstock are models, and such images are being used for illustrative purposes only.

Certain stock imagery © Thinkstock.

ISBN: 978-1-4582-0251-2 (sc)
ISBN: 978-1-4582-0253-6 (hc)
ISBN: 978-1-4582-0252-9 (e)

Library of Congress Control Number: 2012903957

Printed in the United States of America

Abbott Press rev. date: 07/09/2012

METAMORPHOSIS

Once more the leaves changed too soon
But will they ever change again?
Or will laws
We can't know now
Send them to the clouds,
Drive them on to heaven
No, further than heaven.
And keep them forever—
The same.
And green.

Jim Good
March 7, 2001

TABLE OF CONTENTS

PART I

THE MOVE 1

SAM AND THE BLUE STREAK 23

FEELING THE SPIRIT 37

FROM SEGREGATION TO INTEGRATION TO
SEGREGATION 49

GOING TO CONWAY 89

QUESTIONS 107

CONFRONTATIONS 121

SEEKING VERIFICATION 149

PART II

REVELATIONS 171

PART III

CODA 185

NOTES

List of Photographs

BAGLEY DOWNS HOUSING DEVELOPMENT, JAN 1944 64

CRESTON SCHOOL BEFORE THE FIRE 76

CRESTON SCHOOL FIRE 77

SCHOOL HOUSE, REPUBLICAN, ARKANSAS 106

BLACKSMITH SHOP, REPUBLICAN, ARKANSAS 119

JAMES L. GOOD FAMILY, NOV 1948, CONWAY, ARKANSAS 159

PREFACE

I lived in segregated as well as integrated Christian societies before the age of ten and I interacted with adult role models, including preachers, who promoted and defended each of the societies. I was confused by the mixed messages and earnestly questioned which society was the right one according to God's will. This initial question about society began a long journey that led to other questions about God. And I asked—is there anything about God, anything at all that can be verified? My journey was a meandering one that embraced elements of religion, science, philosophy, and spirituality but I found my answers by the time I was 35. And as a result of what proved to be a fortuitous near-death experience, I also found what my life's Purpose should be by the same age.

* * * * *

When I read a memoir, I always question how much of it is really true. Now that I've written one, I have a better appreciation of the inherent difficulty in knowing the answer to that question. This memoir is true according to my memory but that can be different from what is really true since my memory is imperfect. And my task was made unusually difficult because of the unusually large number of places I have lived, 31 addresses by the age of 20, and the number of schools I attended—13 from the first through the twelfth grade. To help verify my memory of events, I sent rough drafts to the other few remaining people who were also witnesses and I've made corrections when they pointed out errors. I have also posted queries on Internet message boards for assistance and I am grateful to have received helpful clarifications. But I've also been encouraged to find that overall my memory of the span of my life covered by this memoir, age five through thirty-five is, I believe, very accurate.

There are caveats:

- I have used actual names for the immediate members of my family, my pets and the names of places I lived and the schools

I attended. I have used fictional names for everyone else and for some churches. And I have dramatized and consolidated some events without affecting accuracy.

- In some cases the original dialogs impacted me with such emotion that they have remained vivid in my memory and are repeated verbatim herein. In other cases I don't have a verbatim memory but I do remember (and can still feel) their emotional impact. In those cases, I have written to convey the emotional truth.

ACKNOWLEDGEMENTS

I am fortunate to have many special friends who've encouraged me to write this memoir and then helped me with the writing. I'm very pleased to extend thanks to:

Al and Valle are two of the special friends. They've shown great interest in my life experiences for many years and have encouraged me to put them into words. Additionally, Al and I have shared long car trips where we talked about our experiences, his in Kansas, and mine in Arkansas, Washington and Oregon. I benefited from his natural keen insight plus his specialized training as a top-notch psychologist. He helped me see some events clearly that had been blurred. I'm grateful that Al and Valle were there at the beginning of this adventure and for reading and constructively commenting on several rough drafts.

Nicki, another special friend, has read the rough draft of every chapter and not only pointed out punctuation and grammatical errors but also made comments that prompted me to rewrite some segments. We have exchanged writings for over 20 years and I've always been inspired and impressed by her writings that are virtually flawless (mine aren't, but Nicki has helped me become better.)

Roger is a long time friend and professional psychologist and I also consider him an expert on religion. He read the rough draft of several chapters and made insightful comments. His comments on Chapter 2, "Sam and the Blue Streak," were especially helpful.

Dick has been a soul mate since the time we met in 1963 and we've walked the spiritual path together as we explored the Mystery. Much of the time Dick has been several steps ahead but he has always taken the time to teach and inspire me. I'm appreciative that Dick gave me the OK to use one of his many observations in chapter nine, "Revelations," and for his comments on chapter one, "The Move."

My lady friend Janet read the rough draft of each chapter as soon as I completed them and was the second person to read the rough draft book. Her on-going encouragement and comments have been very helpful. She also had the special challenge of tolerating my mood swings as I wrote the book. Like most people, I've had some very painful experiences and when I wrote about them, I relived them to a surprising extent and that adversely affected my moods as well as those around me.

It's been very encouraging to receive help from people who I've never met in person—but through Internet websites, forums, and emails. I searched for many months to no avail to find a photo that would be reminiscent of the Arkansas shacks I lived in as a young boy. Fortunately, I finally discovered the wonderful photos in the "Arkansas and Mississippi Delta Blues" collection that can be seen by visiting www.padrephotography.com. One photo in this collection, "Getting By," was it! I knew immediately that it was the photo that would be exactly right for my front cover so I asked the owner and photographer, Brent C. Powell, for permission to use it and he graciously granted it. He also gave me permission to do some editing of the photo, and I have. I encourage everyone to see his complete gallery and to see "Getting By" in its unedited form. It is well worth a visit.

Thanks to Lynita Langley-Ware, Director, and Don Williams, Researcher, of the Faulkner County Museum in Conway, Arkansas for sending me several photos of the few buildings that were in the small community of Republican, Arkansas at one time. With permission, I've used one of them in chapter five and one in chapter six. In addition, Lynita helped clarify some historical details about Republican and Don sent me useful information about property our family owned in Liberty and Conway, Arkansas.

I'm very appreciative of the vital contribution that Jimmy Bryant, Director of Archives at the University of Central Arkansas, made to my research. There was very little public information about our family's forced move by the army from our farm in WWII but Jimmy through his contacts was able to add to it. Chapter one, "The Move," describes my recollection of this traumatic event. It's also important to note that Jimmy is the author of the excellent history book, *The Centennial History of the University of Central Arkansas*. This institution was known as the Arkansas State Teachers College (ASTC) when I lived there in 1948-49 and attended its Training School in the eighth grade as described in Chapter Eight, "Seeking Verification." ASTC also played a major role in the education of my parents, brother Bill, and sister-in-law, Mary, who were students there.

Shirley Souders and Jan Fenter gave exceptional help by answering queries I placed on the Ormultno Internet message board hosted by Rootsweb. Shirley gave me a photograph of the Creston School in Portland, Oregon as it appeared before it was totally destroyed in a 1944 fire. Thanks to her generosity and permission I've used it in chapter four, "From Segregation to Integration to Segregation." Jan solved a puzzling question I had regarding the name of the school I attended when I lived in Vancouver, Washington in 1943. Her analysis was shrewd, thorough and very professional.

My thanks to my immediate family who helped me:

Laura, my former wife; my daughter Marian Gallagher and son James Lester Good III. I'm especially grateful to Laura for helping with chapter nine, "Revelations," and for Marian's help with chapter one, "The Move."

My sister-in-law, Mary Lowe Good made helpful comments about chapter ten, "Coda." Mary is in a unique position to have made the comments—she is the only other person known to me that witnessed my father's funeral described in chapter ten.

My nieces Lisa Good and Jeanne Good: Lisa is one of the strongest supporters of our family history research and came through with encouragement many times when it was needed. Jeanne, also a strong supporter, was the first person to read the rough draft book and made several useful corrections and comments.

CHAPTER 1

The Move

THE BROWN AND green lizard scurried from the shade of the cottonwood tree and headed to a small hole in the side of our corncrib. I had interrupted its nap by claiming the shade tree for myself and it ran across our lumps-of-clay front yard made oven hot by the Arkansas sun. I watched the tip of its tail disappear in the hole and thought for a moment of running over and forcing it out with a long stick that lay at my feet. It was too hot though so I just sat and stared at the corncrib and the small crop of cotton that was growing just beyond. There were some insects flying and buzzing about and an occasional cluck from one of our chickens and in the distance a very strange dust cloud was gathering. There was also a sound I had never heard before—a low rumble that I could not only hear but also feel. Believing that the dust and noise had some connection, I concentrated on the cloud and watched it move slowly toward me along the dirt road that ran in front of our farm. It was like a large ghost that grew larger, thicker and more ominous. The cloud moved real slow but finally it was so close I could make out what caused it. Army trucks were on the move.

Our farm was about two miles from the small community of Cato and about 10 miles from Little Rock, the capital of Arkansas and its largest city. Its 40 acres were without doubt among the most beleaguered in the state with no redeeming traits whatsoever. The soil was poor quality with high clay content that became hard in warm weather, slick when it rained and frozen in cold weather. A few bitter weeds grew here and there along with a type of very formidable, wire-like grass and wild onions. Our two cows, Pet and Lou, had a hard time living off the "pasture" and they frequently repaid our hospitality by producing only small amounts of milk laced with the odor and with the taste of bitter weeds and wild onions. What the farm lacked in good soil it made up for with a very bad community of pests including all sorts of flies, spiders, tarantulas, scorpions, chiggers, and other crawly things that had no name. The largest population though was mosquitoes that were so thick that when they covered our cows, as they did every evening, our yellow cow looked the same color as our black one until you got up close. Some neighboring farmers kept large, smoky fires burning in their pastures so the cows could stand in the smoke to help drive the mosquitoes away. Dad didn't think the fires were a good idea though because it made the cows "soft in character" and the more mosquitoes on the cows, the fewer there would be on us or as he said, "The cows are sorta like fly paper." And there were snakes: copper heads, water moccasins and many kinds of non-poisonous snakes that lived wherever they pleased. We kept a hoe on our front porch so we could easily grab it and carry it with us to kill snakes when we walked the 50 yards or so to our mailbox. But while our farm was not good for farming, it and our neighboring farms did have the right stuff to make an ideal base for soldiers undergoing training. The U.S. Army thought so too and seized our farm through the process of eminent domain promising us a fair price and agreeing to move us wherever we wanted for free. It was 1941, World War II was raging and the American military forces were growing and their facilities were expanding. Our farm and our entire community including cemeteries and the Mt. Pisgah School disappeared and became part of Camp Joseph T. Robinson located just north of Little Rock, Arkansas. Camp Robinson was a multi-purpose camp providing artillery training, bombing practice and specialized facilities to hold up to 4,000 German prisoners. Just prior to World War II it was comprised of 6,000 acres but by leasing and eminent domain proceedings it grew to 44,000 acres by war's end. At its peak it was in effect the second largest city in Arkansas with an average daily population of 50,000. The people displaced for the Camp Robinson expansion, including our Good family, were generally very poor with few resources and given little time to pack up and move.

The army trucks were stirring up the dust cloud and causing the rumble with their large tires, six to a truck. I was just learning to count and could count pretty good up to 100 so as the trucks appeared single file from the cloud, I was pretty sure there were twelve of them. Some stopped and parked in front of our farm and others turned onto the trail that led from the road to our barn. When they were all parked, the drivers as if by some signal stopped their engines and looked toward the house and then at me. I counted two soldiers in the cab of each truck but the truck beds were covered with a green canvas and I guessed more solders might be in the back but I couldn't be sure. An "L" shaped pattern of trucks surrounded me. I wished my mother or father or even my sister Joan, five years older than me, was there but they were working in the backfields picking cotton. I had been left to play alone because I was still one year short of the age of six, which was the age when kids were expected to start working in the fields. I had listened to my parents talk at the supper table about seeing army trucks and soldiers when they went to town. It was, sighed my mother, "because of the war." A war that some bad person named Hitler had started. I wasn't sure where Hitler lived but I thought it might be in the scary farmhouse way down the road, the one with weeds in the front and a flour sack curtain that blew in and out of a front window. I didn't understand much about a war but I heard that it caused people to get captured and killed. The war terrified my mother because my two older brothers, J.C. and Bill, would probably be sent down the road to fight Hitler.

I had seen an army truck before because an occasional one would drive down our road and disappear over the hill. Not even the grown-ups knew why they came or where they were going. This time was different, though. There was not just one truck but a lot of trucks and all parked on our farm with the soldiers looking at me.

I guessed that the soldiers were sent to capture me and the rest of my family and that it had something to do with the war and Hitler. I wondered if they would kill us like I had seen Dad kill chickens by holding onto their heads and twirling their bodies until their necks snapped off. The thought of having my neck snapped off really scared me but I was too afraid to run. Instead I sat under the tree looking at the trucks and the soldiers, not moving from their trucks, looked back at me. I put my head on my arms and bowed my head downward until it touched my knees. Mostly the only thing I could see then was the ground just beneath me. But by shifting my head slightly and rolling my eyes I could see our farmhouse out of the corner of my right eye and from the corner of my left eye I could see the trucks parked in the lane that led to our barn. I figured that my best chance for staying alive was to do what I had seen a possum do. Only last week while going with Dad to empty a rabbit trap, I was surprised to see not a rabbit but some other type of animal with a toothy grin on its face and a long skinny tail that reminded me of a big mouse. "It's a possum sure enough," Dad said and I saw that it was dead. When Dad opened the trap, the possum didn't move and when he poked it with a stick, it still didn't move. Our hound, Charlie, came up and growled, sniffed and nibbled at the possum but I knew it wouldn't move because it was dead. Dad must have guessed what I thought because he said, "He's not dead; he's playing dead. That's what they do when they're cornered. Come on let's walk away." So, we walked a good distance away from the trap and then turned and looked back. "Now watch," Dad said. I looked as closely as I could but I didn't see anything except the dead possum lying next to the trap. Then, slowly there was a movement and the possum got up and lumbered to a nearby tree, climbed it and disappeared from sight. I had learned how to act if I ever got trapped.

I heard a truck door open and the sound of two soldiers jumping to the ground. Then, I heard the crunch of clay clods as they walked the distance to the front of our house. One soldier knocked on the door and then moved back in anticipation of it being opened. They waited a few minutes and when they got no response, the soldier stepped forward again and knocked louder this time and yelled, "Mr. Good?" A few moments later both soldiers knocked and yelled, "Mr. Good? Mrs. Good?" After a while they decided no one was going to answer, so they stopped knocking and yelling and started talking to each other. I was watching all of this with my head still down, not moving and hoping they wouldn't pay any attention to me. But one soldier pointed toward me and I figured since no one answered the door that they would walk over to the tree, capture me and then snap my neck off. And they started walking toward me and their boots stirred up dust and crunched some of the clay clods.

The soldiers came close and stopped just where I could, from the corner of my eyes, make out their boots and their legs up to about their knees. Remembering how the possum acted, I decided to close my eyes tight, fall over on my side and stop breathing. Maybe then the soldiers wouldn't waste their time capturing me and just go away.

"Son, son? You OK, son?" one of the soldiers asked.
"I think he's having a fit," the other one said.
"Ain't no fit. When people have fits, they roll around, stuff comes outta their mouth and they say funny things. My Aunt Emma, now, she has fits and this boy sure ain't actin like Aunt Emma does."
"Then what's he doing?"
"Well, he ain't moving that's for sure but I don't know what exactly he's doin."

One of the soldiers shook my shoulder and then nudged me with his boot. I didn't move or open my eyes but I did have to take a breath so I took as small a one as I could. I hoped the soldiers couldn't see me do it.
"I don't know what's going on with this boy but let's just leave him alone and start putting stuff in the trucks. We'll start with the cows and mules and then move the stuff from the house. Don't know where his parents are but let's start anyway. We got our orders."
As the soldiers walked back toward the trucks, engines were started and I heard some of the trucks driving off and leaving another dust cloud as they rolled down the road. I waited until I thought all of them had left and then slowly I moved my body so I could look where they had been parked. But not all of the trucks did leave. Five of them, the ones in the lane, were still there and soldiers were hopping out of the back and heading toward the barn. The soldier who had knocked on the door yelled, "Start with the mules—put them in the last two trucks. One apiece."
"Junior, why are you on the ground like that?" It was the voice of Dad. I had been so busy watching the soldiers while playing dead like a possum that I hadn't heard him come up from behind. I didn't like being called "Junior" but since I was named after my Dad, I expected it and everyone in our family called me that.
"Are you all right, why are you on the ground?" he asked with more urgency and some anger.
I stood up and looked at him and saw that Mom and my sister Joan were also there.

"I didn't wanta be captured so I did like the possum did that we saw down in the pasture the other day. I laid on the ground and played dead."

"These soldiers aren't gonna capture you—the soldiers are here to move us." He said with a mixture of astonishment and anger.

Joan couldn't contain herself and she chanted in a really mocking way, "Junior is gonna get captured! Junior is gonna get captured!" The mocking way she chanted the words, I knew she would be doing it over and over again for a long, long time. And she would tell the neighbor kids and they would chant it too and then everyone would laugh.

"I didn't know we were moving," I said. I was talking softly to the ground because I was too scared to talk to Dad directly, but I hoped he would overhear me.

He did.

"You didn't have to know about the move–that's for grown-ups to know about and to worry about. All you gotta do is stay in the shade and play. Next year you'll be out in the fields with us pickin cotton and helpin with other things. Then you'll know a lot more than you do now. You should be thankful that all you gotta do now is play. Your time is comin soon enough. Now get out of the way and stay out of the way."

I thought I was already out of the way but I double-checked where I was sitting and moved even closer to the trunk of the tree. Then I was positive that I was out of the way.

Mom had overheard what Dad had said to me. She walked over and looked down at me with an expression of frustration and fatigue. She was sweating from her day of picking cotton and something was worrying her.

"Yes," she said, "We're movin but I didn't want to tell you–didn't want to worry you none and wasn't sure you'd understand. But those soldiers are gonna load up the things in the house and our animals and then they'll take them to our new farm."

"Then, what's gonna happen to us?"

"Well," she said with a sigh, "We're goin in one of the trucks to our new farm. Then a few days after we leave here, the army is gonna fly over and drop bombs on this farm and our neighbors' farms; our neighbors are being moved too. All this you see will be a bombin range

THE MOVE

and a shootin range where the Army will practice fightin so when they go off to the real fightin they'll be good at it." This made me happy because my oldest brother, J.C., had left home recently to be an Air Corps pilot and he was right at that moment at an air base in Texas being trained. It seemed to me that it would be a lot better to have our farm bombed by someone in our family rather than by a stranger.

"Now you just sit and stay outta the sun and stay outta the way of the soldiers. I'm goin over to the house and help pack up things. After a while I'll come get you and we'll get in one of the trucks. Nothing to worry about—just stay out of the way and don't get in the sun."

Four soldiers were pulling and pushing our gray mule Pete to the back of the first truck. Pete didn't like it and gave a baleful bray and balked. It didn't do him much good, though, and the soldiers were able to force him to the back of the truck where a wooden ramp led from the ground to the inside of the truck. Two soldiers moved to inside the truck and pulled on Pete with a rope while the other two soldiers pushed on Pete's rear end and hit him with a stick. With an extra-loud bray, Pete stopped resisting and moved rapidly inside the truck—so rapidly that the first two soldiers were trapped in the truck with Pete who now was real mad and scared. He bucked, gnashed his teeth, kicked his rear legs and shook his head from side to side. He was making an awful racket every time his feet hit the truck floor. The two soldiers at Pete's head were able to open the canvas in the front of the truck bed and escape by crawling up on top of the truck cab but not before Pete had nipped them in their legs and rear ends.

"We gotta move that other mule a different way," one soldier said as he rubbed his rear end.

And they did move our second mule, a brown one named Tobe, a very different way. They added reinforcements—two more soldiers. Three soldiers pulled on long ropes while standing on top of the truck cab while three other soldiers pushed from the sides and behind. Moving Tobe inside of the second truck turned out to not be very hard because Tobe had a much gentler nature than Pete. And it also helped a lot that the soldiers had been taught some important lessons by Pete.

Our two cows, Pet and Lou, were moved next and they were much easier to load in the truck than the mules. The cows were gentle enough so that two of them shared one truck, the third truck in line.

Then, I watched the furnishings from the house being moved and placed in the fourth truck. It didn't take long for the soldiers to empty the house. There were several empty potato sacks that had been filled with clothes and miscellaneous items. Four beds had been disassembled and moved as well as four mattresses, ten cane bottom chairs, a rocking chair, pots and pans and a few dishes. There were also several wooden orange crates filled with books, a few tools and some seeds that would be used at the next crop planting time. The books were Bibles and hymnbooks that Dad had borrowed from several churches that he had attended over the years. He planned to return them some day but never did and he didn't think Jesus would mind because they were borrowed for Jesus' sake. Mom didn't agree to him "borrowing" the church books and once during a heated argument told him that what he did was just plain stealing. He shouted to her, "It isn't stealin when you're stealin for Jesus and, besides, nothing but good has come of it and I'm gonna return them someday anyway!" Mom didn't have a rebuttal to his argument or at least she didn't say anything but I could tell by the look on her face that she still didn't agree with him. Dad would use the books on Sundays when he decided to conduct church services at home rather than go to a church where the preacher didn't preach the way he wanted. He would assemble us on the front porch and pass each of us our very own hymnbook and Bible that had our name written inside the front cover. I couldn't read but I was told that if I looked at the words long enough I would understand them some day. In the meantime I was told to remember the words of the hymns in my heart and when it came time for singing, to "just sing along" and sing along right. As an incentive to sing along right, Dad would sometimes stand at my left, place his right hand on my right shoulder and hold some of my hair loosely in his hand. If I missed too many words, he would yank my hair. It was a teaching technique that worked real good and I soon learned the words to several hymns. We would sing a few hymns and Dad would choose the selections based on what mood he was in. One of the songs he almost always chose was *The Old Rugged Cross* because he said it was important to remind everyone that we were all going to die someday. When the singing was finished, Dad would read from his Bible while those in the family that could read would follow along in their Bible.

THE MOVE

The Bible was even more important than the hymnbooks because it explained about the life of Jesus and what God and Jesus wanted us to do. Since the grown-ups read the Bible to learn important things, I wanted to read it too and although I had been given my very own, I still couldn't read it no matter how hard I tried.

Before the crates could be placed in the truck, Dad remembered something important, walked over to the tool crate and got a hammer from it. He then hurried to the house, made a few banging noises and came out of the house holding yet another orange crate. This crate was empty and it was the only one that had a curtain. It had been nailed to the kitchen wall and had been used as a combination medicine cabinet and dish holder. Dad had pried it off the wall and now held it proudly; "We'll use this at our next farm——it's as good as new," he told Mom. She was pleased too since she had made the curtain out of a flour sack and didn't want to make another one. Mom was very good at making things out of flour sacks including shirts, blouses, and underwear in addition to curtains and tablecloths. She favored the *Magic Millers* brand because the flour sacks came in several patterns. She was particularly fond of the pattern she used on the orange crate curtain, a sky blue color with small white flowers on it.

We almost never had oranges to eat, but we had an arrangement with the Piggly Wiggly store in the closest town to give us their empty crates and in return we agreed to do all our grocery buying at Piggly Wiggly and none at all at their competitors. It didn't take too long before we had more crates than we needed for storing so we used the extra ones for fire wood. They burned real good.

The soldiers completed the packing, and the sergeant in charge walked over to Mom and Dad and told them that it was time to go. Mom was surprised at this and told him, "There're things left in the house we need to move. There's a stove in the kitchen and one in the living room. We've got three kettles in the back yard to wash our clothes in. And we've got plows, harnesses and food for the animals."

"Mrs. Good, the stoves have gotta be left in the house. They're a mess to move with them all being full of soot and ashes and the Government is gonna give you enough money to buy new ones—new ones much better than you got now. And the plows, harnesses and all those other things you mentioned—well, they're packed and in the fourth truck over yonder. You just didn't notice that we already packed them."

"I noticed," Dad said "And, you might think it's time to go all right but we aren't gonna go 'till I make sure we get our money. It would be just like the Government to come in, kick us and our neighbors outta our homes, use our farms for bombing practice and then not pay us. I want our money! I want what's coming to us and I want it right now!"

The sergeant handed Dad an envelope. "Here's a check from the Government. It's the money to buy your farm, pay for the things we didn't pack up and the crops you've picked. There's a little extra money too. You'll find it's the money we agreed to and more. We told you we'd treat you right."

Dad pulled his pocketknife from his pants and opened the envelope. "Come here, Tish!" Dad only used the affectionate name, "Tish," for Mom when he was happy so I guessed that he liked the check. The two of them studied it, turned it over and studied the other side and then looked at each other, said a few words, smiled and nodded their heads. "OK, now we can git going," Dad told the sergeant and then he said with a shout, "Everyone use the toilet 'cause it'll be a long time before we stop!"

My sister Joan being a girl always had first call on our two-seater outhouse. Even so, I sometimes raced her for it just for fun. It didn't do any good though because she always won. Then she would turn and stick her tongue out at me before she closed the door. It was too hot to do any running so I just headed toward the barn with Dad walking close behind me. Mom stayed by the house since she only went to the toilet at night. She didn't go to either the outhouse or barn in the daytime because someone might see her. "It's not ladylike for women being seen walkin to the toilet," she would say, "With men and boys, it's different." Mom was even a bit concerned that Joan could be seen because even though Joan was only 10 years old, she was fast becoming a woman in Mom's eyes. Mom thought about calling her back right then and there but she decided to hold her tongue for another year or so.

After leaving the barn, I decided to take one last look at the inside of our house but first I took off my hat. When we went outside in the summer time, we wore a straw hat with a broad brim to help reduce sunburn and sunstroke. And the hats also had air holes in the crown to help cool our heads but they didn't seem to do much good. When we went inside, we were expected to take off our hats because only heathens wore them inside.

I knew that the inside would be even hotter than the outside so I left the back door open and opened some windows. It didn't matter anymore if flies and other insects came in because the house was going to be bombed anyway. I was struck by how different the house, now mostly empty, was. It not only looked different but it smelled different and as soon as I walked inside I could tell that it sounded different too. The planks creaked louder and in a different way when I walked on them.

Our house had a living room, a kitchen and one bedroom. There were no closets but nails were nailed in all the walls to hold clothes, towels, pots and pans and anything else that needed to be kept out of the way. There were so many nails driven in the walls that our house had become porcupine-like.

I went to the living room, and slowly circled the pot-bellied stove. The sides of the stove would glow red in the wintertime when the firewood, especially pine wood, was burning at its peak. Now it was black with gray patches, cool to the touch and it had been cool since last winter, several months ago. There were a few pieces of firewood and some kindling stacked in the corner of the living room ready for the coming winter. A large can that was dented on one side was on the top of the stove. In the winter, it was filled with water that evaporated as the stove got hot making the air more moist and comfortable. Looking at the stovetop, I was also reminded that Dad, as a special treat, would sometimes put peanuts in the shell on the top to roast. It was a challenge to remove the peanuts at the right time—too late would mean burnt peanuts and too soon would mean raw peanuts. It was easy to get fingers burned while removing the peanuts—that's why only Dad was allowed to roast them.

In front of the stove and close to the front door, a piece of linoleum had been nailed to the floor to cover a crack. Looking through this crack had been a lot of fun. Our house rested on columns two feet tall located at each corner—otherwise there was no foundation. It was built like that because if floodwater ever reached the house, it

BORROWED BIBLES

would flow right under it and do no harm. All the other farmhouses around us rested on columns too. Our community was prepared for a flood even though no one remembered one ever happening as long as anyone could remember and that was a good 60 years. Maybe the reason there had been no floods was because the nearest river was more than 10 miles away but God could get mad at us any minute and the grown-ups said he was good at making floods. Anyway, the house on columns design created a large open space under the house that stayed cool even in the hottest weather and it would have been a wonderful place to play except for all the crawly things that lived and slithered there. There were mice, ants, spiders, scorpions, snakes and quite a few other crawly things that had no name. It was fun, though, to be inside the house and look down through the crack in the floor and watch all the crawly things scurry by and go about their business. And no matter how hot the rest of the house got, there was always air from the crack and it was always cool. A bad thing about the crack though was that the crawly things would sometimes come through it into our house—the ants traveled in convoys marching along like disciplined palace guards straight ahead looking neither right nor left. The spiders and the nameless things came alone, came cautiously and looked right and left and also over their shoulders. The things could be scary and unsanitary. I was told that they would track all kinds of nasty stuff and diseases into the house. Mom would get real upset by them so she talked Dad in covering up the largest crack, my favorite peephole, in the living room as well as another crack in the bedroom. He found a piece of linoleum and nailed it on top of the cracks. For good measure, he placed our rocking chair on top of the linoleum-covered crack in the living room. "This'll keep it down." And now that the rocking chair had been moved to the truck, the linoleum glistened and stood out like sunbeams off a puddle of water. I ripped it from the floor and threw it to the side of the room where Mom and Dad's bed used to be. I had given the crawly things their freedom and imagined that they would be lined up waiting anxiously to rush into the living room. Nothing moved, however, except for a wisp of cool air that coiled its way into the room. Maybe they were waiting for nighttime when they would enter all sneaky like. If that's what they were doing, they sure would be disappointed to find no one to bite and no food to eat and nothing to carry back to their nests. Later, some would be killed in the bombing. The crawly things had once been our enemies but we had come to a kind of truce when the linoleum had been nailed to the floor. It was a demarcation line. It was ironic that they would take over our house with my approval and assistance only to have it, and some of them, destroyed by the bombing.

I ran. I ran around the living room stove—slowly at first, but then as fast as I could. I ran in wider circles, over to the firewood stacked in the corner, over to the place where Mom and Dad's bed had been and then over to my peephole crack. I jumped up and down on it. I ran to the bedroom, jumped over the places where our three beds had been; beds where my two sisters, two brothers and I had slept. I ran into the kitchen and touched the wall where the orange crate medicine cabinet had been. As I ran, I made sure that I touched each and every nail in the house that I could reach. I thought that if I touched all of them, the experience would be burned into me forever and that's what I wanted: I wanted to remember our house on this day forever. Then I went to the noisiest floor planks and jumped on them and jumped on them and jumped on them until I was worn out from jumping. I had never been allowed to run or jump in the house when we lived in it so I took advantage of its emptiness and ran and jumped as much as I pleased. And it was not nearly as much fun as I thought it would be. I left the house and rejoined Mom, Joan and Dad and the soldiers outside.

"Now I heard you runnin and jumpin in the house," Mom said with impatience, "did you get enough? Did you get it out of your system?" This was the kind of question that she didn't want or expect an answer to. Of course, it wasn't a question at all but Mom's roundabout way of saying she didn't like what I did. Even if I had wanted to answer her, I wouldn't have had the chance because she rapidly changed the subject within one breath and added, "Well, it's time to go. Our things are loaded in the trucks and we gotta go now."

"My name is Luther and I'll be helping you all into the truck." It was the voice of one of the soldiers and he directed his words to Mom and me. As the three of us walked to the back of the first truck I saw that Joan was already in it and sitting on one of the orange crates that had been turned upside down. Dad was standing on the ground next to the truck and was waiting for us. Luther put together a stack of crates to make a small ladder for Mom to climb on, and with Dad's help, she climbed up the ladder into the truck. Luther picked me up and put me in the truck. Then Dad climbed in and then Luther. "I'm gonna ride back here with you all to make sure everything goes all right," Luther said. Then he closed the tailgate from inside and sat on the floor.

I suddenly realized that Charlie wasn't in the truck with us. In fact, I hadn't seen Charlie being packed up and I asked, "Where's Charlie?"

"I saw him a while ago, he was runnin through the back woods sniffin and diggin and barkin. He likes to do that you know," Dad said.

"We gotta wait for him!" I said.

"No! We're not gonna wait. We don't take dogs with us when we move. We never have. Too much trouble. It doesn't make sense. Anyway, dogs have a way of takin good care of themselves and he'll be fine. He'll find another home real soon. And we'll find another dog real soon when we get to our new farm."

"But all the homes will be bombed. Then, what'll Charlie do?"

"Didn't you hear me? Dogs have a way of taking good care of themselves," Dad said with finality. When he used that tone, it was over. It wouldn't do any good to argue, to think about arguing, ask questions, or think about asking questions, or to say anything—anything at all. Any more words from me would lead to a whipping, a hair pulling or at least a long scolding.

I had learned that grown-ups were mostly right about things, but Charlie being left behind scared me and I didn't understand how he could be all right when our farm and our neighbors' farms would be bombed. I was afraid he would be killed just like the crawly things under the house. I sure hoped he *did* have a way of taking care of himself, but in any case he was left behind. The chickens were left too, chickens that were interesting individuals not only in looks but also in personality. I felt that they belonged to me since I was the one who had given each of them a name when they were only chicks. The cotton crop that had hijacked so many hours of labor from us—some stolen just today—would also be left. The crawly things were left too (those that had names as well as those that didn't) but I had sort of said good-bye to them when I was in the empty house so it wasn't so bad. I never did learn what happened to the chickens or the cotton crop or to Charlie.

THE MOVE

It's a good thing that our body has learned how and when to release a sedative into our blood stream. It's a special sedative that helps tolerate events that are extremely sad, extremely scary, and extremely painful. It helps to tolerate these events but it doesn't erase them. After being assaulted with the surprise visit of the soldiers, and learning that our house would be destroyed and learning that we would be leaving Charlie and the chickens behind, my body reacted. It released the sedative. After that, I was dazed. I could see but I looked through eyes that seemed to be covered by an oily film. I could hear but my ears were partially plugged by soldier noise and truck noise. I could feel but my feet had turned to wood. I was only vaguely aware of our truck starting up and driving down the dirt road with the four other trucks following us creating a ghost like dust cloud behind.

The two soldiers in the cab of the second truck waved at us from time to time just for the fun of it. Dad, Joan and Luther would always wave back, especially Joan who not only waved but jumped up and down in a flirty sort of way. I didn't wave because I was too dazed and neither did Mom. She sat still in the truck with her eyes closed and her hands in her lap. Mom called this "dozing" and she did it every chance she got. It was not actually sleeping but her way of taking leave of the rest of us for a while and getting some much needed rest.

Out of the corner of my eye I could see that we were moving past other farmhouses and the cotton crops that were growing on them. I didn't see a single person or any animals and the houses looked empty. The Army had already been there and had moved everyone. Then I saw weeds, huge fields of weeds instead of cotton. I knew then that we would soon pass the house that I thought Hitler lived in, but Mom said he didn't. I hoped she was right because otherwise we might have to stop and fight him. That worried me because we didn't have many soldiers in our small truck convoy and I hadn't seen any guns at all. Soon we passed by the farmhouse and we didn't see anyone, and no one shot at us. Mom was right as usual. Still, I remained a bit concerned because the flour sack curtain in the front window was flapping in and out and I couldn't feel any breeze.

A little bit later we passed by a cemetery that I had seen before and it always scared me. I was told that there were some very old folks buried there dating back to Civil War days. Most of the graves had

15

weeds or briars around them but there was at least one recent burial there because I could see a bouquet of wilted wild flowers on top of fresh dirt. "We've gotta move all those graves, too," Luther said, "and we're gonna start doing it in a day or two. It's gonna be hard work made extra hard cause of the hot weather, and it's gonna be messy, and scary. And it just don't seem right disturbin the restin place of those folks."

"Well, it don't seem right to bomb em either!" Dad said.

"That's a good point, Mr. Good," Luther agreed. "That's a good point!"

We left the dirt road and moved on to an asphalt one. I had never been on an asphalt road before but I had heard that if you took our dirt road far enough you would run into one and we did. I was amazed how smooth our ride became and how we could move so fast and yet not create a dust cloud.

Our truck slowed down and drove into a large road stop with several picnic tables, a small grocery store and a filling station at one end of the stop. The other four trucks arrived and parked behind us and filled up the park, which meant no other cars, or trucks would be able to park in it until we left. Dad and Luther climbed out of our truck and helped Mom and Joan out. I wanted to jump from the truck but that wasn't allowed so Luther helped me out too. Dad and Luther headed toward the store and the rest of us were told to wait and they would buy some food and bring it back to us and then we could have supper. The other soldiers moved to the picnic tables and began to eat food that was in the truck. I heard Luther tell Dad, "Now buy what you want cause the Government is paying for your food tonight."

Dad brought back a stick of bologna, a big loaf of Wonder Bread, onions and some Sandwich Spread that came in a jar with a big mouth. Sandwich Spread was a gooey concoction, yellowish in color with little red and green things in it. I didn't like it very much but we always had it with bologna sandwiches and I was told that if I ate it often enough I would learn to like it. There were also some cupcakes and Royal Crown colas—one for each of us. Despite all the signs that talked about Coca Cola, Dad never bought any because he said it was a sin to drink it. He had learned that there was some higher-up person that worked for Coca Cola that didn't believe in God. That meant Coca Cola was the devil's drink. If Dad wanted to tell you that something was bad, he would say, "It's as bad as Coke." It was one of my secrets that I really wanted to drink one but I didn't dare say so. Joan was tempted too and once whispered in my ear, "Someday I'm gonna get me a Coke and I'm gonna drink it too!"

Another problem with Coca Cola was that it came from Atlanta, Georgia. Royal Crown, RC, on the other hand, was made "right here in Arkansas by good, God-fearing folks that love Jesus." And yet another thing, Royal Crown packed twice as much in a bottle as Coca Cola.

We sat at a park bench far from the other soldiers. Mom and Dad were on one side with Joan and me on the other side and Luther in between us. The hot summer day was ending and being pushed aside by the almost as hot night. Crickets were feeling safe enough to start their evening requiem and the ants and other crawly things started to appear on the tabletop but Luther brushed them off as fast as they appeared. He took it as a challenge and there was a gleam of satisfaction in his eye since he proved to us that he could keep the tabletop clean.

Dad used his pocketknife to cut large slices from the bologna stick and slices from the onion. He passed the slices to Mom. She put one bologna slice and one onion slice on a piece of bread, smothered the slices real good with Sandwich Spread and then put another slice of bread on top. She passed the sandwiches to us along with a Royal Crown and a cupcake. All of us ate our sandwiches as fast as possible so we could get to the cupcakes, a very rare treat. As a matter of fact what we did wasn't really eating in one sense; it was chewing as little as possible with our mouths open as wide as possible and swallowing as much and as fast as we could. Luther seemed stunned by our manners and didn't know how to act or what to say, but after thinking about it for a while he looked at Mom and said, "In all my life I've never had a sandwich with so much Sandwich Spread on it!" She took his comment as a compliment and looked real proud of herself.

Mom was usually the one that finished eating last but this time she was squirming, biting her lip and devouring her food so fast that she finished first, which surprised me. The reason for her unusual behavior was that she hadn't gone to the toilet all day. This was her usual way, but now that it was getting dark she needed to go but couldn't figure out how to do it without the soldiers seeing her walk to the outdoor toilet. Pretty soon, though, the pain became too much. She took a deep breath, got off the bench and headed with Joan to the toilet. She was careful to keep her head down as she walked and she told Joan to do the same. The soldiers couldn't be stopped from looking at her but at least they wouldn't be able to look her or Joan in the eye.

When Mom and Joan returned, Dad got off the bench and walked to the end of the table. He had a serious look on his face and I knew what would happen next. He looked us in the eyes individually, starting with Mom, then moving to Luther, then to Joan and then to me. We did a lot of things according to age in our family and since I was the youngest I got talked to last and looked at last. And I was the last one that was allowed to talk. Joan knew these rules very well and sometimes kept talking, even when she didn't have anything to say, just to make me mad.

Dad finally spoke in his stern, Sunday church voice, "Things went real good today because God was with us. But we got some tough days ahead: a new farm to get working, new people to meet and a war to fight. We'll need God more than ever so we're gonna sing a church song and I'm gonna give you some words outta God's book. Now Luther, I want you to go over there where the rest of the soldiers are and ask them if they want to join in on our service to God." Dad was not an ordained preacher but he often held services at our house anyway.

Luther soon returned and seemed embarrassed that he brought only one soldier whom he introduced as Charles. "All the others are too tired or too busy," said Luther. Actually, it didn't seem that too many were tired because there was a lot of laughter coming from them punctuated with occasional whoops and yells.

Dad said he was going to keep the service short because it had been a long day and everyone was tired. And it didn't matter that more soldiers weren't going to join us because that was God's will. "We'll sing *The Old Rugged Cross*," said Dad as he passed out the hymnbooks. "And as we sing, remember how our Savior suffered for us and that we're gonna die and join up with Him someday—that is, if we've lived a good Christian life."

We had all heard the hymn many times including Luther and Charles and our hymnbooks were so worn that it was easy for me to find the song in the book even though I couldn't read. And it was easy to sing especially since we could just follow Dad who had a deep, booming voice and kept time with his fingers for the rest of us who were assembled choir-like in front of him.

I liked the *Old Rugged Cross* better than other hymns because I knew it so well that Dad didn't have to pull my hair to get me to sing it right. And it was uplifting even though it was also scary and mysterious. I was always relieved when we got to the verses toward the end:

> So I'll cherish the old rugged cross,
> till my trophies at last I lay down;
> I will cling to the old rugged cross,
> and exchange it some day for a crown.
>
> To that old rugged cross I will ever be true,
> its shame and reproach gladly bear;
> then He'll call me some day to my home far away,
> where his glory forever I'll share.

We closed our books and Dad resumed talking. "Now we learned in that wonderful hymn that 'He'll call me some day to my home far away where his glory forever I'll share.' Yes, it's true that if we lead a good Christian life, we'll go to heaven after we die, and share the glory of Jesus forever. But if we don't lead a good Christian life, we'll go to hell and share fire and brimstone with Satan forever. Now, how do we lead a good Christian life? We obey the Commandments, follow the Golden Rule, get baptized, and accept Jesus as our savior, that's how. There's one more thing though that I want you, Luther, and you, Charles, to know and that's to choose the church that Christ himself started. Now I'm not saying that other churches can't get you to heaven but why take a chance? Why not go to Christ's church? And what's the name of that church? Well, let's just turn to the Bible and find out cause it's written in there so now just turn to Matthew 16:18."

Embarrassed once again because I didn't know how to read and couldn't find Matthew 16:18, I nudged Mom. She sensed my predicament, and turned the pages of my Bible for me and then whispered, "There," as she pointed to some words on the page. That helped me a little because I could at least look at the right words while Dad read them out loud.

"Now pay close attention to Matthew 16:18," Dad said, and he read, "And I tell you that you are Peter, and on this rock I will build my church, and the gates of Hades will not overcome it."

Dad looked intently at Luther and Charles and said, "All right, now who was it that said 'On this rock I will build my church'? Luther looked at the ground and didn't say anything but Charles shouted, "Why, it was Jesus that said that! Yes sir, it was Jesus!"

"Right, it was Jesus but Jesus is a name, and an important name at that but lots of folks had Jesus as a name but what was his title? A title that only He can claim."

"Why, it's Christ, that's His title!" Charles exclaimed with a proud look on his face.

"You bet, it was Christ talkin and it was Christ that said He would build His church so the church that He built was the Church of Christ! Don't you see?"

Charles said, "Makes sense and I never thought about it that way before just now."

"Well, do either of you belong to the Church of Christ?" asked Dad. Luther looked at the ground and mumbled "no." Charles said, "I'm a Baptist."

"Being a Baptist just might be all right and one thing for sure it's not as bad as being a Catholic or a Methodist." Dad didn't like Catholics because they were led by the Pope who lived overseas and wanted to rule the world and besides they had preachers that wore strange clothes and they did strange things on Christmas Eve. Methodists weren't that bad but they were bad enough. They had become "Yankeefied" and had watered down their teachings so much that it was hard for them to tell right from wrong. Baptists and Presbyterians weren't far wrong but they did allow piano music in church and it was well known that Jesus didn't want pianos playing in His church. For anyone that doubted Jesus' intent, Dad would refer them to the exact verses in Acts, Romans, Ephesians, Colossians and James. Each and every one of those New Testament verses referred to singing only----musical instruments were not mentioned. Yes, there were lots of other churches too but most were too small to matter much one way or the other and it was a good thing because some of them had very strange practices.

Dad continued, "Luther, I don't know what religion you are cause you're not saying much, but when you and Charles get back home, it'd be smart for you two to look up the nearest Church of Christ, talk to the preacher and join. When you think about the differences between heaven and hell, you want as many things on your side as you can get. Do you see?"

"Makes sense," said Charles, "and I'll do it! I'll do it as soon as I get home again." Luther kept looking at the ground and didn't say anything. He was avoiding Dad's stern looks and I could tell that Dad was disgusted with Luther for not speaking.

Dad stretched his right arm high over his head with his palm open; he lowered his eyes and said, "Let's pray." I always had mixed feelings when he did this. On one hand, I felt good because I knew the service was about to end and sometimes he said some interesting things in his prayers. I felt bad though because sometimes it seemed like he had more to say than all the words in the Bible put together and it was hard to sit still for so long. He began by thanking God for showing mercy and not killing everyone during the big flood, he gave thanks for loving us so much that he gave His only son to die for our sins, he thanked God for seeing that the Government paid him a fair price to bomb our farm, and he asked God to look out for his two sons, J.C. who was in the Army Air Corps and Bill, who was in the Civilian Conservation Corps, and to look out for his daughter, Marie, who had recently moved away from home and was living who knew where. He thanked God for the Army men who were moving us to our new farm and gave special thanks to God for Luther and Charles and hoped God would lead them to the Church of Christ. He didn't ask God to do anything for Mom, Joan or me and I suppose the reason was that we were still at home and didn't need any extra protection. Finally, Dad lowered his arm, said, "Amen," shook Luther and Charles' hands, collected the hymnbooks and Bibles and walked away to be by himself.

"Now it's time for us to turn in and go to bed," Mom said to Joan and me and led the way to the Army trucks. The soldiers were going to sleep on the ground and let our family sleep in the truck cabs. It was understood that Mom and Joan would use one truck, Dad would use another and as a special treat I would get a truck cab all by myself but I had to promise not to play with any of the knobs or the steering wheel or anything else. It was an easy promise to keep because I was so tired.

Through the side window of the truck I saw soldiers asleep on tarps and Dad in the distance standing alone. I heard the sound of a dog barking and was relieved that it didn't sound like Charlie. These were my last memories of the first day of The Move and the beginning of continuous memories of my life. I was five years old and in some sense my life began when the trucks arrived. Prior memories were no more than disjointed glimmers.

CHAPTER 2

Sam and the Blue Streak

IT HAD BEEN a little over a year since the Army, obeying an eminent domain order, moved us to our farm close to Lonoke, Arkansas. We named it Steel Bridge after a nearby bridge that was noteworthy for the area because it wasn't made of wood. And just like our old farm, Steel Bridge had no running water, electricity or telephone. Our lighting was from coal oil (kerosene) lamps.

The move had been made much easier by the care that Luther had given us and he continued to act as a thoughtful friend of our family. We never saw him again but he sent Joan and me a birthday card, the first one I ever received, and for Christmas 1941 he sent our family a Christmas card. In turn, Dad and Mom sent Luther a Christmas card with a note thanking him again for his help, wishing him well and wondering if he had joined the Church of Christ yet. Luther never did answer that question.

Christmas in 1941 was memorable for another reason—I received my first Christmas present. Our brother J.C. sent Joan and me presents that Mom and Dad wrapped in newspapers and gave to us after breakfast. I unwrapped mine in a hurry, jumped up and down and shouted with excitement when I saw the metal truck painted bright red with black, shiny tires. From that time on until I wore it out over a year later, I pushed the truck around the floor and looked for things to put in it and move from one room to another. I tied a string to its front bumper so I could pull it all over the farm loaded with rocks. But in my imagination they weren't rocks; they were farm animals, bales of hay or sometimes they were soldiers going off to battle and I was their commanding officer. Joan was just as happy when she unwrapped her Raggedy Ann doll that she named Bertha after one of Mom's sisters. She was learning to sew and from that point on she saved scraps of cloth to make into doll clothes. Once Joan started to make Bertha a pair of slacks but Mom stopped her because her doll was a Raggedy Ann and not a Raggedy Andy and the Bible said that women shouldn't wear men's clothes. Joan stopped making slacks and made dresses instead.

We didn't have money to buy presents or decorations so Christmas day was usually very ordinary—except for the coconut. About a week before Christmas, Dad was always able to buy a coconut no matter how little money we had or how remotely we lived. He would place it in the corner of the living room so we could look at it but he gave orders not to play with it or even touch it. Then, just before we went to bed on Christmas evening, he would puncture the eyes of the coconut and pour each of us some of the milk. After we drank it, he would use a hammer to break the coconut into small pieces and give us each some of the pieces that contained the meat. The meat was crunchy and chewy and I didn't like it very much; however, Dad really enjoyed it and ate what the rest of us didn't. I never heard of anyone else that had this custom of eating coconut on Christmas but Mom said it started the year they got married in 1918. It continued until Dad's death in 1971.

It didn't take me long to get used to our new farm because for both good and bad reasons it was similar to our old one that was about fifty miles away. The soil was almost as poor but there were patches of pretty good dirt here and there. And it was just as overrun with all kinds of pests and if anything, the snakes were worse. As Mom sadly noted, "If it's bad, Steel Bridge has got it." It did have a small pond, however, which made watering our cattle somewhat easier. The problem was that the pond was pretty shallow so it dried up if the weather stayed hot for very long. And during the year we lived there, it got much hotter than usual according to our neighbors. But Dad used the hot weather as the basis of a church service he held on our front porch one Sunday. After gathering Mom, Joan and me on the porch, he passed out our hymnbooks and Bibles, raised his right hand and asked God to bless the service he was about to conduct. We then sang the *Old Rugged Cross* and after we finished, Dad said it was OK for us to sit down. He cleared his throat and said the weather sure was hot but it was nothing compared to the heat of hell. And the hot weather should be a reminder to us to lead good Christian lives so that when we die, the devil won't come get us and take us to hell. The heat isn't all we would have to put up with either—there would be screaming and yelling from all the millions of other people in hell and there would be a terrible smell like nothing we had ever smelled before. And once we were there, we would never be able to leave; we would be there forever. On the other hand, if we obeyed the Commandments, accepted Jesus as Lord and got baptized then we would go to heaven when we die and we would be there forever, but that would be all right because we wouldn't want to leave. In heaven we would always be happy, never sick and there would be plenty of milk and honey. And we would also be able to talk directly to God, to Jesus, to the angels and other good Christians. Dad then read the Ten Commandments to us while we looked at them in our Bibles; he specifically emphasized to Joan and me that one of the Commandments was for us to honor our parents. Dad ended his sermon by saying that from then on when we complained about the hot weather, we should be thankful we weren't in hell and to make sure that we behave so the devil won't ever come to carry us down there. Then, he told us to stand and sing *I'll Fly Away* so we would get a feeling just how happy we're going to be when we die and go to heaven. Mom helped me find the hymn in my book and we sang:

> Some bright morning when this life is o'er
> I'll fly away
> To that home on God's celestial shore
> I'll fly away.
>
> I'll fly away, oh Glory
> I'll fly away in the morning
> When I die Hallelujah, by and by
> I'll fly away.

Dad told us to keep standing and bow our heads while he said a closing prayer. He raised his right hand and asked God to watch over us as well as his two sons, J.C. and Bill, who were in the Armed Forces, and to bring cooler weather and rain. Then, he told us he had finished the service and for Joan and me to sit and be quiet for the rest of the day, and especially not to laugh. Sunday was God's special day and we were expected to be somber.

Steel Bridge had a lot of crisscrossed paths that had been made by the previous owners and wild animals. That made it easy to explore including otherwise inaccessible briar patches and poison oak patches. One day I was walking with Mom on one of these paths that led from our pond, through a briar patch, through our cow pasture and then to our barn. Our cows, Pet and Lou, had stopped grazing and were looking at us with curious but wary eyes. Then, seeming to recognize us, they went back to grazing on a patch of "bitter weeds"—one of the few plants not killed by the recent hot weather. For the past few weeks the milk from the cows had been hard to drink because the weeds made it taste and smell so bitter. Even so, we were better off than some neighboring farmers whose cows had gone completely dry.

Our barn looked far away and I guessed that it was going to be a while before we reached it because we were walking so slowly. "Let's hurry," I said, "it's red hot out here. "Well, that's exactly why we don't hurry. Folks can get sunstroke if they hurry in this weather." Mom replied.

I didn't know very much about sunstroke even though Mom talked about it a lot. And, whenever she talked about it, she always slowed down whatever she was doing and expected the same of me. She started to walk even slower but I wanted to get to the barn in the worst way so I could play in the hayloft. It would be cooler in the loft and I wanted to finish building the fort I was making out of hay bales. I decided to see if I could get her to run because that would hurry things up and I knew I could beat her in a race. I had never seen her run but I could see me running fast and leaving her behind and that would make her proud of me and she would think that I was grown up. Besides, I had two secret weapons that I had thought of that would let me run faster than anybody. I figured that if I ever got in a race with someone and needed to run faster, I would run three or four steps and then jump one giant step, leaving them behind for sure. And, if I needed to, I could go even faster yet by holding my arms out straight and flapping them like roosters did.

"Mom, let's run," I said as I jumped up and down in anticipation of beating her.

"It's too hot," she answered, "besides I don't want to run off and leave you."

"But I can run faster than you, I just know it."

I was sure I would get to the barn first and then I would look back and wave to her, and then we would both laugh.

"Come on," I pleaded.

I expected her to keep arguing with me but to my surprise she started running. After some distance, she looked back, slowed down a little and yelled over her shoulder, "Well, come on, and let's run."

At first I ran slow, thinking that even my slow speed would be fast enough to catch her, but it wasn't. So, I ran faster and faster and soon I was running as fast as I could but to my surprise I still couldn't catch her. Then, I tried out my secret of running and then jumping but I got farther and farther behind. I put my arms out and flapped them as fast as I could while I ran and jumped, but I still couldn't run as fast as she could. It was hard to see clearly through my tears of frustration but I knew that she was getting ever farther away and was almost to the barn. I threw myself on the dusty path while the sun beat down on the back of my head. After a while, I felt a hand on my shoulder and Mom said, "Come on, we can run again another time and it won't be long before you beat me." I slowly raised myself up and noticed two small mud holes formed by my tears mixing with the dust. My front was dirty and I felt humiliated, defeated and I thought my life had been ruined. Mom took my hand and squeezed it while I stumbled along and occasionally gave way to tears.

We were close to the barn when she stopped and let go of my hand. She stared at a patch of weeds to our right and not far off the path. I still couldn't see very well because my eyes were red from all the crying I had done, but I wiped my eyes with my hand and studied the patch of weeds that got her attention. Then, I was able to make out a dog lying there on its side and not moving. We walked closer and I could see that it was the black and white hound dog that lived on one of the farms close by. It often came to our farm to run and sniff around and to play with me a bit. Its teeth were hanging over its lips that now had a strange black color and there were all sorts of insects crawling over its body. I will never forget the dog's eyes. They were shut and it looked like the eyelids had grown together and then been covered with molasses. We hadn't noticed the dog when we walked down to the pond, but as if to answer my question, Mom said, "It's been dead three or four days I reckon." I had seen dead ants and things like that lots of times and once I saw a dead lizard and a possum that played dead but I had never before seen anything dead that I had known. Why it was only a few days ago that he came over and ran around our trees sniffing at something. And sometimes our dogs, Penny and Fanny, would join him and the three dogs would run off in a pack and explore the trails. I never did learn his real name or where he lived exactly but I called him Sam and he seemed to like it. I would call his name and whistle and he would come to me. After we played a bit, he would return to sniffing and running until he was out of sight. I felt sad when I imagined what it would be like not having him to play with anymore and I was scared when I looked at his eyes. And I remembered Charlie, our dog that we left behind at our old farm.

"Why does that happen, Mom? I mean his eyes . . ."

"When animals die, their eyes shut. Sometimes they die cause they're sick and sometimes just cause they're old and it's their time. It's the natural way and then they begin to rot."

"How about us when we die?"

"Yes," she said with sadness, "when we get old enough, our eyes will close too and we . . ."

She sighed and shook her head slowly back and forth, which told me that her thoughts made her too sad to finish explaining.

"And then what happens after we die, is Dad and the preacher right? Do we go to heaven?"

"Well, if we've been good, we go to heaven and we get to see Jesus and God and all the angels, but if we've been bad-—well, if we've been bad, then the devil will come and get us like your Dad said and carry us back to the place below and we'll burn in flames forever and ever. And don't ever say, 'die' in front of your Dad cause it'll make him real sad and real mad."

"Is 'the place below' the same as what the preacher calls hell?"

"Yes, but that's a word we don't use in this family unless we're real careful about it. Do you understand? Instead of that word we call it 'the place below.' And if we talk about folks we don't say 'die' we say 'gone away,' but it's OK to say 'die' if we talk about critters."

I didn't understand and said, "But Dad said 'hell' last Sunday when he talked about how hot it was."

"That's different cause he used it in a sermon. Then it's OK and you'll hear preachers use it that way too. Now, that's enough questions for right now. Let's get to the house. I've got to start a fire and fix supper. When your Dad comes in from the field, I'll ask him to bury the dog."

"His name is Sam," I said.

We returned to walking on the path and soon we passed by the barn. Only a little while ago I wanted to get to the barn real bad, but now I barely looked its way. I didn't want to play in it anymore or play anywhere else either for that matter. I just wanted to get to the house and sit on the front porch and think. Losing the race to Mom still bothered me a little but that memory was getting dimmer because I was mainly thinking about Sam and his eyes. The memory of him looking at me with molasses eyes made me sad and it also scared me.

Our farmhouse was about fifty yards from the barn. It had two bedrooms so Mom and Dad had their own while Joan, Marie and I and sometimes my brothers used the other. In addition, it had a living room, a kitchen, a front porch and a back porch with cane bottom chairs on both porches. We would often sit in the chairs in the summer evenings and wait for the house to cool off; otherwise, the inside would be too hot to sleep in. We also sat in the chairs on the Sundays that Dad conducted church services. In the living room there was a wood-burning stove to provide heat, a few chairs and a bed for guests; however, I don't believe we ever had guests. There was also a small table that held a battery-powered radio. The batteries would last about three months—we could only afford to buy batteries once a year, right after we sold our cotton crop in September. And behind the stove on a nail was a razor strap that Dad used to sharpen the straight blade of his razor, but the strap also had a more ominous purpose: Dad sometimes used it when he whipped someone. I saw him use it to whip Mom and Marie and he brought both of them to tears. I was told that he had also used the razor strap on both J.C. and Bill when they were children but if so, that was before I was born. When Dad calmed down after the razor strap episodes, he seemed to feel bad about them but also justified. He felt it was his duty and right to dole out tough punishment because the Bible said that the man was the lord over his wife and that a child would be spoiled if the rod were spared. For some reason, he never used the razor strap on me. Instead, I was made to cut my own switch from one of the trees and bring it to him. If he didn't like what I brought him, he made me go cut another one. I learned that he favored a switch about three feet long and about one eighth of an inch thick so that it would "sing and sting" when he whipped me with it. He went easy on Joan the few times he whipped her—he just gave her bottom a few gentle whacks with his hand.

If Marie was home, she, Joan and I slept in one bed in one of the bedrooms. If either of my two brothers were at home, a second bed would be placed in this room. Nails had been driven into the bedroom and living room walls to hang our clothes on.

The kitchen had a table, chairs and a hardwood-burning cook stove. Next to the stove was a box where ashes were kept. Some of the hardwood ashes would be mixed with hog fat to make lye soap to wash our clothes, our hands and anything else Mom decided to wash. Orange crates nailed to the kitchen wall were used as a pantry. One special crate with curtains that Dad had brought from the old farm was used to hold what little medicine we had: a bottle of turpentine for external aches and pains and a bottle of "Black Draught" for internal aches and pains ("Black Draught makes you smile from the inside out.") There were more nails in the kitchen walls to hang things on and a can of coal oil was kept in a kitchen corner to sterilize cuts and bruises.

I walked through the house and went straight to our front porch with its four cane bottom chairs. The chair seats were sagging; two of them seriously so, because they were about a year beyond the time the cane should have been replaced. I sat in the chair with the best bottom, put my head in my hands and looked at our front yard and out toward the dirt road that connected our farm to the nearest town of Lonoke a few miles away. Our dogs, Penny, a part collie and Fanny, a part bulldog, were snoozing a few feet from my chair. Most farms had only hounds of some type so our dogs were very unusual. They came to us one Saturday when a car stopped in front of our house; the driver got out and threw a potato sack on our front yard with Penny and Fanny inside. It was not unusual for folks who lived in Lonoke to put unwanted pups or kittens in a sack and throw them on nearby farms so we were used to it. And Dad would take the sack, kill the animals inside with a hammer, and bury them on the farm. He decided to let

Penny and Fanny live, however, because of the especially appealing way that Fanny could whine. They were self-sufficient and ate whatever scraps of food we might have left over and whatever they could find on their own.

From the front porch, I could easily hear Mom in the kitchen talking to Joan and to my oldest sister Marie, who had come home for a short visit. Marie asked Mom what was wrong with me because I had come through the house without saying anything. And Joan commented that I was dirtier than usual and looked sick. Mom answered, "He saw that dog that he plays with, the one he calls Sam, and the dog was dead. It's lying down in that weed path just beyond the barn. That really scared him and he's dirty cause he fell on the dusty part of the path." Thankfully, she didn't tell them about the race that I lost and my tears.

I sat there listening to Mom and my sisters talking and all of a sudden I realized that, just like Sam, they would be dead some day too. My two brothers would be dead and Dad would be dead. Every one of the chickens that were walking on the farm looking for insects would be dead. The new baby on the farm up the road would be dead even though it was so young now. And even all the preachers would be dead no matter how good they were and how hard they prayed. Every thing living now would be dead later. When I realized this, I was overcome with fear, sadness and anger but also determination. It seemed wrong and sad that everything, good or bad, was going to die. There should be a way to stop all the dying and I decided I would find a way.

"Supper!" Mom yelled, and I knew she was yelling for me because Dad, Joan and Marie were already sitting at the kitchen table and eating. I sat down, crumbled some corn bread in a glass, poured milk over it and slowly ate it with a spoon even though the milk was so bitter I could smell the bitterness. We hadn't had any meat for several days and everything in the vegetable garden had died in the recent drought. We had eggs and biscuits for breakfast and corn bread and milk for dinner, the noon meal, as well as for supper, the evening meal.

"I don't know what we'll do if the cows go dry, like some of the neighbors' cows have," Mom said.

"Well," Dad said with exasperation, "we'll just eat bread until hog killing time comes in a couple of weeks."

Although I hadn't had a lot of food the last few days, I wasn't very hungry because I was sad and scared knowing that everyone of us at the table was going to die.

"How old will we be when we die?" I asked. As soon as I asked the question, I knew I had made a big mistake because Mom had just warned me not to talk about dying especially in front of Dad. While I hadn't asked anyone in particular I expected Dad to answer because I knew in our family we spoke in order of age.

Dad's face turned red, his breathing got heavy, and he almost gagged on the cornbread in his mouth.

"Don't ever speak about us dying!" he shouted at me. "We don't use that word in this family. We say 'gone away,' do you understand? I don't know what got into you to ask such a question as that."

"But, Dad, most everyday you go away and go to work somewhere but you always come back."

"That's a different kind of thing and you know it! Are you trying to sass me? You're gettin a blue streak in you!"

He didn't say anything else but continued to look at me as he ate and his face got redder and redder. I took my spoon and poked the cornbread in the glass of milk but I didn't feel like eating at all anymore. And in addition to everything else, I started to worry about the blue streak that I was getting in me. I had learned from listening to Dad that people could get two kinds of streaks: yellow and blue. I knew that a yellow streak meant that you were a coward but I didn't know what a blue streak was. I only knew it wasn't good.

After supper, Dad went to sit on the front porch and dip snuff. Mom and my sisters stayed in the kitchen to wash the dishes. It was a bit early but I decided to go to the bedroom and lie on the bed before my sisters came in so I could have some peace and quiet. Later, when all three of us were in bed, it would be hard to concentrate on figuring out a way to stop all the dying and that was what I had to do.

I hung my overalls on a nail and lay down on the right side of the bed in my union suit. When my sisters came in, Joan would lie next to me and Marie would lie on the other side of the bed. They always talked to each other for a while before they went to sleep but they never talked to me so their talking just made me mad and kept me awake.

I lay there and looked at the ceiling and found my favorite knothole to concentrate on. I was very tired but I had learned a lot. I had learned that in our family we didn't say "hell" or "die." I learned that I was getting a blue streak in me and that flapping my arms didn't make me run faster. I also learned that all living things die and when they do, their eyes close. I thought of Sam again and Charlie and the vow that I made to myself to find a way to stop all the dying.

Then, I discovered the answer! It was going to be easier to stop dying than I had first thought. I reasoned that all living things closed their eyes when they died so I simply would never close my eyes ever again and then I wouldn't die. So, I stared at the knothole without closing my eyes as long as I could but I found that no matter what I did, one of my eyes would close out of habit. I figured that I could get around this, for a while anyway, by only staring with one eye while the other eye rested and then I would switch eyes very carefully so both of them were never closed at the same time. This seemed to work but I didn't know if God would consider it the same as having both eyes always open at the same time. But, for the time being it was the best I could do and maybe with practice I could learn to always keep them both open at the same time. I wondered, though, what would happen when I slept? I didn't know if my eyes closed when I slept or not but I hoped that if one or both of my eyes were open when I fell asleep, then they would stay that way while I slept.

It was almost dark when my sisters came in and noticed me with my eyes wide open. Marie said, "Why are you staring at us like that? I thought you'd be asleep by now." I didn't answer her and rolled on my side and rested first one eye and then the other, being very careful not to close both eyes at the same time. My sisters talked to each other as if I wasn't there and giggled like they usually did.

When it got dark, my sisters stopped talking and I could tell by their breathing that they were both asleep. I rolled on my back and stared at the ceiling but it was too dark to make out any details such as my favorite knothole. So I held out my arm and stared at the palm of my hand first with one eye and then the other. This worked almost as well as staring at the ceiling.

The bedroom door slowly opened and a big man, even bigger than Dad, walked in holding a staff in his left hand. He didn't hesitate at all but walked directly to my side of the bed. He had a terrible odor—the worst that I had ever smelled. He leaned over put his face close to mine and looked at me through sealed eyelids smeared with molasses. I tried to scream and wake somebody but I couldn't get any sounds out of my mouth and Marie and Joan stayed asleep. "I came to get you!" he said. Then, he picked me up, threw me over his shoulder and walked through our house without waking Mom or Dad and took me to the back yard. I realized that it was the devil that had me and he was taking me to the place below and I couldn't do anything about it. I had explored our back yard in detail and never noticed anything unusual but the devil pointed his staff to a patch of weeds and a large hole opened up. He jumped in it with me still over his shoulder and that caused me to see everything upside down. We were falling and going faster and faster and although he didn't say anything, he laughed as we fell. I could see that we were headed toward flames and there was an awful odor coming from them—the same smell that the devil had. As far as I could see in every direction, there were flames and I could hear hundreds, maybe thousands, of people screaming. It took a long time but we finally stopped falling and the devil grabbed me, pulled me from his shoulder and put me down in flames that came up to my waist. He put his face close to mine again to make sure I saw his sealed eyelids smeared with molasses. Then he spoke, "You died, and I came and got you cause of that blue streak in you!"

I woke up still frightened by my dream. Now, I was even more determined than ever that I didn't want to die so I immediately started staring again without closing my eyes. I dressed and went into the kitchen. Dad had already left to do some plowing and Marie and Joan were out picking blackberries. There was one fried egg left on the egg platter and several biscuits.

"Eat up," Mom said, "we've got to walk down to the pond again. And why are you staring at everything like that?"

I didn't answer her but I turned my head so she couldn't see my eyes and quickly ate the egg and all the biscuits.

As we walked through the back yard, I took a moment to investigate the patch of weeds that the devil had turned into a tunnel opening in my dream but it looked the same as always. Then, we continued on the path and past the barn and the weed patch where we had found Sam but he wasn't there. I guessed Dad had buried him but I didn't ask because I didn't feel like talking about Sam.

I was bothered by knowing that I had a blue streak in me while at the same time, I didn't even know what a blue streak was. I was also scared since so far I couldn't help blinking my eyes no matter how hard I had tried and that meant that I would die unless I learned some way to keep my eyes open.

"Mom, how did I get this blue streak in me?"

"You don't have a blue streak, son. You're too young for that. Your dad was just talking like that cause you made him real mad."

"Why'd he get so mad?"

"Your dad's afraid of dying and he won't allow anyone to talk about it, especially at the supper table."

"Well, what does having a blue streak mean?"

"I don't know either. I just know it isn't good but your dad always gets mad when I ask him exactly what it means."

It made me feel better to know that I didn't have a blue streak, and someday maybe I would find out what it meant but, then, maybe not since Mom didn't know either.

"If I learn to keep my eyes open all the time, will I still die?"

"Yes, you will, but you don't have to worry about that for a long, long time. You're just a little boy and your whole life is in front of you."

"But, I thought you said that everything closes its eyes when it dies. So, if I never close my eyes, how come I'll still die?"

"Well, I didn't mean that everyone closes their eyes when they die. Some folks do die with their eyes open, but then other folks come up and close their eyelids before they're buried."

She paused and then continued, "Like your Dad said last Sunday, we have to be real good so we can go to heaven and live forever up there since we can't live forever down here."

I reached up, grabbed her hand and squeezed it. It was going to be another hot day, even hotter than yesterday, and I was not going to ask her to run again and I was not going to ask any more questions for a while. I had learned that always keeping our eyes

BORROWED BIBLES

open wouldn't stop us from dying but if we were good enough we'd go to heaven and live forever anyway. And that was a good thing because Mom and Dad and my brothers and sisters were getting old it seemed to me.

CHAPTER 3

Feeling the Spirit

WE STAYED AT Steel Bridge for about two years and it was a very formative time. We were fortunate enough to have a school bus route close by so I caught the bus into the town of Lonoke where I attended the first grade. It was my first entry into any kind of society and I was constantly amazed—especially with electric lights and running water. Throw a switch and there's the light, no coal oil, and no wicks. Don't worry about knocking the lamp over and starting a fire. Don't worry about burning the house down. Just throw the switch and watch in amazement but keep your fingers out of the socket. And running water? Just as amazing. Imagine a toilet in the house where you sleep and eat! Yes, rich folks had toilets inside their houses and used special store-bought toilet paper—not newspapers, catalogs or corncobs. Yes, special paper made just for toilets. Amazing!

Mrs. Sarah West was the Lonoke first grade teacher and she proudly and regularly told us that she was half Caddo Indian. It seems her father had been a land speculator who was making his rounds through Texas when he became acquainted with a tribe of Caddo Indians and tried to barter with them. The bartering didn't amount to anything but in the process he met a young Indian woman that caught his fancy and after a brief courtship and the payment of a proper dowry they were married. Sarah was their only child and both parents doted on her and taught her the ways of the Caddo as well as the white man. Sarah grew up in Texas but her marriage brought her to Arkansas where she earned a college degree and a teaching credential. She labored hard to teach her first graders not only the alphabet and other basic information but also the ways of the Indian. She explained that the Caddo could walk all day and not get tired like the white man simply because they put one foot in front of the other in a neat line, not like the raggedy way the white man walked. To drive this lesson home, she had us walk down a line she had drawn in the hallway while she looked closely at our feet and chanted, "Stand up straight! Walk straight! Walk, walk, walk!" Soon, walking in a straight line like a Caddo became second nature and it really did help my endurance. Throughout the school year, she also brought different kinds of berries and leaves and showed us what was good to eat and what was poisonous and how to make specialty teas out of certain leaves that would cure chills, lower fevers or thin the blood. She claimed that the Indians were wiser than the white man because they could make a tea that would cure cancer but she never got around to showing us how to make that one. Once she made a paste out of leaves and told us the paste could be used to spread on cuts and bruises to bring down swelling and "suck out the poison."

The time spent with Mrs. West was very enjoyable and educational and I looked forward to each hour spent in her classroom. Unfortunately, the school day also had recesses and a lunch period and those times were very painful because of harassment from the other kids.

The racial makeup of the first grade reflected the segregated society of Arkansas in the 1940s. Although the surrounding area of Lonoke had a large black population, none were in my school nor were any other races except white. But there was lots of diversity in wealth and because of this diversity, I learned something—we were very poor! Joan and I were the children of poor farmers and this put us in a social class below the children of professional workers as well as blue-collar workers. We were substantially below the children of rich plantation owners who were at the very top of the pecking order. There were other kids in the school who were also poor but they didn't draw the same attention as we did partly because we were the new family in a community that almost never had new families and partly because Dad insisted that we take good care of the outside of our farm house. But by doing this, the community thought we were being uppity since we painted our house with whitewash—a mixture of lime, water and salt—while everyone else let their houses remain unpainted and weathered. And unlike others, we didn't use flattened tobacco cans to plug holes in the outside walls and we kept the screens in the windows clean and tight. This maintenance required almost no money and made our house look better but it also made us the community misfits.

"Hey, Uppity! Hey, Whitewash! Yeah, you, Uppity Whitewash!" the kids chanted as they circled me on the playground. And these weren't just first graders but kids all the way up to grade six, the highest grade in our school. They did the same to Joan too and sometimes alternated their Whitewash chant with "Hey, Flour Sack—show us your flour sacks!" because somehow they had learned that she wore underwear that Mom had made from flour sacks. And the fact that Joan's underwear and my shirt was made from the same Magic Miller's Best flour sack pattern was obvious and led to a lot of laughter and taunting. Fortunately, there were some other kids that wore flour sack clothes and they, at least, didn't join these particular taunts but they did join in others.

The seven-mile bus ride to and from school was over a dirt road with gravel spread here and there but it didn't do much to keep the dust down and when it rained, the gravel was washed away anyway. We would pass over the small bridge made of steel that our farm was named for and over a gully that was so deep that the bus had to slow to a crawl to pass over it. There wasn't much else to see except a couple of other farmhouses, wild blackberry thickets along the side of the road and cotton crops. Just south of the town of Lonoke we passed by a huge fish hatchery that was the world's largest, covering over 200 acres. There were a lot of weeping willow trees planted around it and it was like a beautiful park where people would gather for picture taking and other events. There was an ugly side to the hatchery though because it was also a massive breeding ground for mosquitoes. The locals often said that, "There's gotta be over a million fish in there," and then someone else would say, "Yep, and over a thousand million mosquitoes!" The mosquitoes blackened the sky every night as they flew out to suck the blood out of us as well as our cattle. The mosquitoes were even thicker than they had been at our farm near Cato from where the Army had moved us. They were so bad that Dad had relented and built big smoky bonfires in the pastures to drive the mosquitoes away, but he still worried that this might somehow spoil the character of our cattle and weaken their natural resistance to diseases.

The ride to and from school was not very scenic but it was very traumatic. The other kids on the bus guaranteed that. When Joan or I would try to take a seat, the space would disappear because some kid would move into it or cover it up with books and coats. "It's taken!" they would shout and follow through with laughter. They wanted us to stay in our place and they had decided our place was standing in the aisle. Sometimes the driver would stop the bus, make the kids stop tormenting us and help us take a seat. But that could make things worse for us because of the retaliation; slaps on the back of the head and kicks to the shins. Then, toward the end of the trip home when our house came into view, a chant that I had learned only too well would begin: "Whitewash, whitewash, whitewash!"

I always had special and mixed feelings about the ending of the Friday school day. I was happy because the coming weekend meant there would be two days when I wouldn't be taunted but I was also sad since I wouldn't be with Mrs. West. I would miss her teaching the traditional first grade subjects but most of all her very special way of teaching the ways of the Indian.

Saturdays were usually spent doing chores with Dad, and if there were any spare time left after the chores, I would sit on the floor in the corner of our bedroom and read the Bible or some other book. It was different if it rained. Then, unless Mom needed some extra help in the house, I would be able to read most all day and I was encouraged to do it. Between what Mrs. West had taught me at school and what I had learned on my own by reading Bibles and hymn books that Dad had borrowed, I was able to read about as well as most kids much older than me. If I did get stuck on a word or a meaning, I would ask Dad or Mom for help but even with their help I didn't understand much about the Bible although I read it a lot. And they sometimes disagreed on what the Bible meant anyway partly because Dad's Church of Christ beliefs differed with Mom's beliefs she had learned in hard shell Baptist churches. Dad said that parts of the Old Testament weren't true because they were the Law of Moses and were changed by the Law of Jesus as recorded in the New Testament. Mom would reply that Jesus himself said that "I have not come to abolish the Laws but to fulfill them," and she could quote the exact verse in Matthew to back up her belief. And she would ask Dad how he could tell which parts of the Old Testament were true and which weren't and that to be on the safe side we should assume that everything in the Bible was true. Mom never did change her beliefs but to keep peace in the family she usually joined Dad no matter what church he went to. And whether it was important or not, I found the Old Testament puzzling but exciting to read and spent more time with it than the New Testament. All the battles, the talking snake and the big flood in Genesis, and the talking donkey in Numbers especially fascinated me.

I also enjoyed reading the textbooks that Joan brought home from school. I sometimes asked her to explain her homework to me and she would if she was in a good mood. I enjoyed looking at her algebra book that she called "wooly" instead of "algebra" because it was so hard for her to understand. While I didn't understand the mathematical symbols that were in the book, there was something about them that was compelling. Sometimes I would copy them over and over again because I believed that if I copied them and looked at them long enough, I would slowly begin to understand equations just as I had learned words by looking at the Bible a lot and asking questions. Saturday was my favorite day because I usually had time to read, especially if it rained.

And it was on an early Saturday afternoon that Mr. Charles Bryant paid us an unannounced visit. It was unusual to have anyone visit us and we were wary of and even scared of visitors. We were especially wary of unannounced visitors but this didn't apply to Mr. Bryant's case because we heard his Ford with a muffler problem a long way away. And then when he pulled in the lane beside our house and cut the engine, it backfired as if to emphatically announce his arrival. Dad had plenty of time to plant himself on the front porch with arms crossed to wait for and challenge his arrival. And Mom had plenty of time to fetch our rifle from its hiding place and load it. Then, she stood behind the closed front door with rifle in hand to back up Dad in case there was any trouble from this stranger. Joan and I stood beside Mom but close enough to the door so we could hear.

"How you do? I'm Deacon Bryant of the Piney Church of God. I'd like to talk to you a bit about our Lord Jesus. Will you allow me some time?"

When Mom heard that it was a man of God that had come to visit, she relaxed, put the rifle down and gave Joan and me a reassuring nod of her head. She whispered to me that I could go on the front porch and join Dad but she made me promise to not say anything.

BORROWED BIBLES

Dad said, "Well, come right on up here and have a sit. Yes Sir, I'm ready to hear what you got to say about Jesus."

"We've got a wonderful church a few miles away up on Piney Road and it's full of God fearing Christian folks and we want you to join us tomorrow. Come share our love of God and Jesus. Now I know you're new here and I don't know what church you belong to but—"

Dad interrupted him and said firmly, "My family belongs to the Church of Christ but there isn't one around here so I've been conducting services for my wife and children myself every Sunday. Now before we go any further, I've been wondering, isn't your Piney Church of God really the Holy Roller church?"

"Well, I know some folks call us that, but we're the Church of God. Now we might do some rollin and we might speak in tongues when the Holy Spirit moves us cause that's just another way we worship God but we worship Him in more ways than just rollin. And let me tell you, if folks understood why we roll on the floor, they would roll on it too!"

"It doesn't seem right to speak in tongues and roll around on the floor. Seems like a heathen habit to me." Dad said.

"That's cause you haven't been to our church and seen it for yourself and felt it for yourself. Now speaking in tongues is the purest thing you can do cause it's the language of Heaven. Other languages come from just plain ol' manmade countries, English comes from England and French comes from France, but talking in tongues comes from Heaven. It's a language we speak but never learned cause there's no learning it, and there's no need to learn it, cause there's just the Holy Spirit guiding us moment to moment. And remember, the Apostle Paul wants us to speak in tongues. Do you remember that he said 'He who speaks in tongues edifies himself---I would like every one of you to speak in tongues' Do you remember Paul saying that?"

Dad had to admit that the Deacon was right. He remembered what Paul said but mumbled that it still seemed like something only heathens would do.

"And as for the rollin," Deacon Bryant continued, "well, when you're speaking the language of Heaven, it's easy for the Holy Spirit to enter you and fill you with ecstasy and you'll just naturally dance around with joy and you'll just naturally fall to the floor and roll. It's just natural!

Anyhow, we'd like you and your family to come tomorrow and see for yourselves. We want you all to come and feel it for yourselves! Now, our service starts at 10:00 and you'll be very welcome. Very welcome indeed! How about it?"

Dad said, "Thank you. I'll think about it and talk it over with my wife."

The Deacon thanked Dad for his time, walked to his car and drove away.

Dad opened the front door that had remained closed during his talk with the Deacon and told us, "Tomorrow morning we're gonna walk over to the Piney Church of God and see for ourselves how they do things. It could turn out all right and make us even closer to God but we'll have to see for ourselves. Anyway, it's around five miles through the back woods so we'll have to leave early to get there when the preachin starts at 10:00."

Joan was able to get out of a lot of chores and commitments by saying that she was sick. She got sick a lot and sometimes she really was sick but often she was just pretending. Mom could tell when she was pretending and then would make her do chores anyway but Joan had a way with Dad and if she appealed to him, he always took her side. So it wasn't too surprising that on Sunday morning Joan decided that she wasn't going to walk with us to the Church of God. "She's sick," said Dad, "and needs her rest." Mom had a look of dismay at this pronouncement but didn't argue the point directly. As Dad, Mom and I headed out the back door to the church, Mom yelled to Joan with sarcasm in her voice, "Now you rest real good cause we don't want you to over burden yourself. We'll be back before 2:00 and we expect you to be in bed resting. You hear?"

As soon as we entered our back yard we were joined by Penny and Fanny who walked behind me. I was pretty sure they wouldn't walk all the way with us because Fanny's short legs, from her bulldog heritage, would soon tire after about a mile or so. Then, Fanny would stop and rest for a while, turn around and walk back to the house. Penny was larger and could walk further but she usually kept Fanny company and I guessed she would turn around too. Penny and Fanny were good dogs but when it came to exploring or walking I really missed Charlie because he was much more inquisitive. Not only would he have walked all the way with us but he also would have found time to sniff around and maybe even flush out a rabbit.

We were soon on the path through our back woods that would lead to Piney Road. Dad pulled his watch out of his pocket from time to time to make sure we were walking exactly fast enough so we wouldn't be late or too early. Both Dad and Mom considered being late not only bad manners but literally a sin that would be punished by God on judgment day. And a sin committed on Sunday was even worse because it was God's special day. I learned to believe this and got to the point where I could automatically adjust how fast I walked so that I was almost always exactly on time.

We walked in single file because the path through the woods was narrow and when we walked single file, it was a family rule to walk in the order of age. Dad, then, would always be first with Mom second followed by J.C., Marie, Bill, Joan and me. It was September, the weather was moderate and the woods were gorgeous with the trees showing their multi-colored autumn leaves. Even so, Mom and Dad were breathing pretty fast and beginning to tire because of the pace we were keeping and because the woods acted like a green house and made the air still and sticky. And as I expected, Fanny and Penny stopped walking, watched us for a while, and then turned back to the house. I wasn't tired at all and I believed it was because I had been walking like a Caddo Indian the way Mrs. West had taught.

The sound of a car crunching gravel meant that we were close to Piney Road. Soon we got to it, turned right and walked along the shoulder. The air was more pleasant along the road than in the woods and there was a slight breeze that was invigorating. On the other hand, an occasional car would pass us and stir up dust and gravels. One car stopped to ask if we wanted a ride but Dad thanked the driver and declined saying that we enjoyed walking and did it as much as possible. I knew, though, that Dad was embarrassed because we didn't have a car and he was too proud to accept a ride. We did have a wagon and could have hitched our mules, Pete and Tobe, to it and traveled to church that way. But that would've taken more time because we wouldn't have been able to take the short cut through our woods.

When the church came into view about 200 yards away, Dad stopped walking and pulled out his watch. He eyed it carefully and said, "We'll slow way down; otherwise we'll get there too soon." If we arrived too soon, it would be awkward because there would be social pressure to talk to other people and neither Dad nor Mom wanted that. Mom was also worried that the other people, especially the women, would make fun of our homemade clothes even though many of them would be wearing homemade clothes as well. The plan was to arrive at the church just as services started so there wouldn't be any time for social interaction. In addition, we would sit at the back of the church and close to the door so we could leave in a hurry if we wanted to. The plan worked perfectly and we arrived just as the other people were being seated. Deacon Bryant was standing at the door welcoming people. He was very pleased that we had decided to visit and he gave us a warm welcome, shaking Dad's hand vigorously with his two hands. Then, he welcomed Mom and took the time to shake my hand and welcome me. No one else seemed to notice our presence and that was the way Dad and Mom wanted it. We took a seat on the left side of the church that was closest to the door. Mom leaned over and whispered to me, "We might leave real fast so stay ready!"

There was a single aisle that led down the center of the church with four bench seats on each side holding about six people each. There was a large open space between the first row and the end of the building where the members did their rollin, I guessed. Also at the end of the building there was a closed door with a small office behind it for the preacher, Pastor Darrel Martin, and a pulpit and a piano. I had never seen a piano in a church before because the Church of Christ that we had always attended didn't allow musical instruments to be part of its services. Dad and Mom also noticed the piano right away and Dad shook his head in disapproval, "Heathen piano," he mumbled.

Deacon Bryant closed the front door of the church. As he walked up the aisle and passed where we were sitting, he touched Dad on the shoulder as a way to give us another welcome. When he got to the front, he faced the congregation, raised his right arm high in the air, palm open and began:

"In the name of God, amen! On this beautiful day that God has given us, I got some bad news. Pastor Martin, our dear Brother, won't be here this morning. He won't be here to preach the word of God. He won't be here to proclaim the glory of Jesus. He won't be here to

BORROWED BIBLES

welcome the Holy Spirit. Pastor Martin has gone all the way to Little Rock to be with his sick sister. Pastor Martin will be with his sick sister in body but Pastor Martin is with us in spirit this morning. Can you feel it? Say Hallelujah!

Hallelujah!

And who else is here? God is here! And who else is here? Jesus is here! And who else is here? The Holy Spirit is here! Yes, God is here, Jesus is here, and the Holy Spirit---they ARE HERE! Say, Hallelujah!

Hallelujah!

Deacon Bryant pulled off his jacket, placed it on a chair, and continued in a much louder voice:

"And God knows how you're suffering Brother Sanderford. He sees you in that third row sitting with your pretty wife, Eileen, who is suffering too. He knows your pond dried up, He knows about your sick children, He knows about those pains in your back, He knows about your bad cotton crop. And He loves you! And He can help! He parted the waters. He can help! He guided the Israelites. He can help! He gave his only begotten Son. Oh, Sweet Jesus! He can help! Receive the Holy Spirit Brother Sanderford! Receive the Holy Spirit and talk to God! Hear us Sweet Jesus! Hear us Lord!"

At this point a woman leaped from her seat and dashed to the piano, sat down and began a rhythmic pounding of the keys. Several other people stood up, put their arms in the air and danced toward the open space in front of the church. Brother Sanderford and his wife were at the front of the dancers and were shouting "Hallelujah" and "Praise God." This shouting went on for a while and at first I could understand the words but soon Eileen started to make sounds that sort of sounded like talking but I couldn't understand what was happening until Mom whispered to me that she was talking in tongues. The other members of the congregation stopped dancing and shouting and formed a circle around Eileen who kept talking in tongues louder and louder. As she "talked," she danced while holding up one hand high in the air and with the other one she held on to her dress at the waist to keep her underwear from falling off. She would shift hands from time to time making sure that one of her hands was always holding up her underwear.

Deacon Bryant had been quiet while the rest of the congregation was dancing their way to the open space but then he continued:

"Now, the rest of you, receive the Holy Spirit and join Sister Eileen! Right now! Right here! Come over this morning. Don't be starved. Come walk with the Holy Spirit this morning. Come over now! Come over now! Come over now!"

Then, Deacon Bryant sang solo with the piano pulsating frantically:

> *I've got a Lord over yonder,*
> *I've got a Lord over yonder,*
> *I've got a Lord over yonder,*
> *On the other shore.*
> *Oh, some bright day I'll go and see Him,*
> *Some bright day I'll go and see Him,*
> *Some bright day I'll go and see Him,*
> *On the other shore.*
> *Oh, that bright day may be this morning,*
> *That bright day may be this morning,*
> *That bright day may be this morning,*
> *On the other shore.*
> *Won't that be a happy meetin,*
> *Won't that be a happy meetin,*
> *Won't that be a happy meetin,*
> *On the other shore.*

Eileen collapsed to the floor and talked in tongues at the top of her voice while rolling around. Several other women and one man joined her and they all were talking in tongues and rolling.

Mom nudged me urgently and whispered, "We're leaving fast." Dad led the way and we walked out of the church quietly but as fast as we could. I was disappointed and sorry to leave since I found the service fascinating and wanted to know what would happen next. It didn't take us long to get to Piney Road and then I asked, "Why didn't we stay till they finished?"

Dad answered, "They behaved like heathens! I thought we should see for ourselves if this was a church for us since we don't have a Church of Christ but seeing what they did is even worse than I heard about what they did. Playing a piano was bad enough but rollin around on the floor like that and talkin like that! No sir! That's not for us."

Mom added, "And those women weren't ladylike. They were just plain disgusting!"

"But," I said, "I thought the Apostle Paul wanted people to talk in tongues like that."

Dad replied, "He did, but what Paul said isn't the law. Now, if Christ had said it, that would be the law. But just so you'll know, Paul also said women shouldn't talk in church and you can see they did some serious talkin this morning even though it couldn't be understood. So the Pastor and Deacon are pickin and choosin to do what Paul said to do and that's not right. That's not my idea of Christian. Now I know you like readin the Bible so go read more about what Paul said in Corinthians."

"Do heathens have a blue streak in them?" I asked

"They sure do! Now, stop talkin. We've got a long walk to get back to the house and it's gettin hotter."

CHAPTER **4**

From Segregation to Integration to Segregation

AS WORLD WAR II expanded so did the growth of federal government facilities in Arkansas. Five major ordnance plants were constructed at diverse locations near the cities of Camden, El Dorado, Marche, Pine Bluff, and Hope. A sixth plant was built near the city of Jacksonville and only a few miles from our farm, Steel Bridge. It was named the Arkansas Ordnance Plant (AOP) and produced fuses and detonators for bombs. From the time production started in March 1942 to the time the plant closed in August 1945 it had produced over one billion detonators and over 175 million fuses. Most of the workers lived within a 50-mile radius of the plant but some lived much farther away. Transportation to and from the AOP was accomplished by a patchwork of buses, railroad shuttles and private vehicles. Until we could afford to buy a car, Dad, Mom and my oldest sister, Marie, were three of the passengers that were transported by buses that served the country roads surrounding Jacksonville. When they arrived at the plant, they found a self-contained and largely self-sufficient facility that had its own fire department, cafeteria, recreation areas, hospital, maintenance department and newsletter. The plant was fenced, security was tight and plant guards thoroughly patrolled the area. Dad was one of the guards.

When the AOP announced that it would be hiring, Dad and Mom became very excited about the potential benefits but Mom in particular had some concerns about working there. It would mean many changes in our life style.

"How'll we raise this cotton crop we started and how'll we get money for it?" Mom asked.

Dad replied, "We won't tend to it like we normally would. No need to. But we'll still get some money cause it won't all be ruined just a bit smaller that's all. Besides, the money I'll be makin there will be lots more than we can make from this crop. It won't be as hard either. It gets mighty hot out there in the fields and the mosquitoes don't help. Now, if you work too? Well, we'd really be well off and can save some money and buy lots of stuff we can't afford now. And remember that Marie is gonna move back in here in a few days. She's 20 now and a good age to work there in Jacksonville and she said she wants to. I figure we'll charge her some of what she makes to help with upkeep. So if you take my money, and yours and Marie's, then we'll be so well off we can buy most anything. We'll even be able to buy a car some day and wouldn't that be something?"

"That'd be something all right and we can get some store-bought clothes too and some real shoes for Joan and Junior and a piece of furniture or two. I don't know though that they'll even hire us cause we don't know nothing about makin bombs."

"They said they'll teach us how to make bomb parts and anyway I don't think it'll be hard to learn how to build something that just blows up. They'll hire all three of us real quick and they'll be glad to do it."

Dad was right. He and Mom easily got jobs and so did Marie who had returned from wherever she had been. With J.C. and Bill in the armed forces, five members of our family were dedicated to the war effort and we were proud of that. It was unusual to have so many members of one family dedicated to the effort, a fact noted by the local newspaper, *Lonoke Democrat*, which served Lonoke Arkansas and the surrounding area. On October 30, 1942 the paper published an article, "Members of Good Family Fight To Win War, Peace." This article states that, "While James L. Good stands guard at AOP, his hip pocket usually carries the pictures of his two handsome sons who are volunteers in the armed forces. J.C, has won his wings in the air corps and Billy J. is a radio operator in the U.S. Coast Guard. Marie, the oldest daughter, is working on Area 11 while his wife, Isabella, is on Area 12." The article also quotes Dad's wish for the war to end, "We are eager to get back to our farm and peace. That gives me and the whole family a job to do in the war, and we want to get our part of it done as soon as possible."

Dad, Mom and Marie were able to work on different shifts at AOP while Joan and I took on additional farming chores after school. By making these adjustments, we were able to keep the farming going much better than Mom had feared and we raised a pretty good cotton crop after all. We also raised a few small crops for our own consumption including peanuts, feed corn, popcorn, watermelons and a variety of vegetables grown in a small back yard garden.

Thanks to the paychecks earned at the AOP, our financial situation improved significantly and we bought new clothes, a better radio (battery operated because we still didn't have electricity) and new kinds of food. Joan and I also went to a doctor for the first time in our lives for a general check up. The doctor told Mom and Dad that we were generally healthy but advised us to eat more vegetables and not so much fatty food. And we were all excited about the purchase of a car, a 1934 Chevrolet. Now we had our own transportation and were not dependent on buses for a ride to the AOP or anywhere else. Gas was rationed because of the war, however, so we, like everyone else, had to be careful how we used it. But since we had three family members working at the AOP, our gas allotment was adjusted upward to accommodate commuting to and from the plant considered vital to the war effort. We were given a B sticker and that entitled us up to eight gallons of gasoline per week whereas the more common A sticker entitled the car owner to only four gallons per week. There were also C (for doctors), T (for truckers) and X stickers. The latter entitled essential holders to an unlimited supply; "essential holders" included police, firemen and civil defense workers. (A scandal erupted when 200 Congressmen received X stickers that they had approved for themselves.)

Sometimes on Saturday evening Dad would use our new car to drive us into Lonoke to see the sights. He always did the driving since Mom could never figure out how to handle the shifting on cars newer than the Model T Ford that she had mastered. So Mom sat in the front passenger seat while Joan and I sat in the back seat with Joan sitting directly behind Dad. Marie never came on these trips because she felt she was too old and she preferred staying behind and reading one of her romance novels that she bought on a regular basis. I was glad that she stayed home because the car was crowded enough as it was. Anyway, Dad would park the car on as busy a street as he could find in the early evening, somewhere around 6 p.m., and we would sit in the car for about two hours and just watch the people go by on the sidewalk. Dad and Mom enjoyed guessing how much money the people made, how old they were and what religion they were. "That person must be 90 if he's a day," Mom once said about a man all bent over and wrinkly. "Not only that," said Dad, "I bet he's pretty lonesome. And I feel sorry for him—in a few years we'll be like that." If someone looked happy, then that person was presumed to be a member of the Church of Christ, but if they looked sad or sick, then they probably belonged to some other church. Dad and Mom and Joan paid special attention to the black folks that walked by to see how they behaved and to see if they were staying in their place. It was in these car trips as well as in school that I learned some of the rules of segregation. I had already learned that the blacks had separate schools and churches. And when I visited Lonoke, I learned that they also had separate bathrooms, drinking fountains, and separate places on the buses and trains to sit. The restaurants that allowed blacks, and some didn't, had a separate area to eat in and a separate entry door, usually in the back. If a movie theater had a balcony, the whites sat on the main floor and the blacks sat in the balcony. If there was no balcony, the whites sat in the front rows and the blacks in the back rows. Interestingly, there were more complex rules too. For instance, there was a black couple that would pass by our farm from time to time in a mule drawn wagon and if Dad happened to be in the front yard it was OK for the man to stop the wagon and talk to Dad. Sometimes he would be invited to sit on the porch (but never invited into the house), would be given a glass of water and he and Dad would share a plug of tobacco or dip of snuff as they talked about the weather and shared ideas on raising crops. All the while, the black woman was expected to stay in the wagon. Black women were not to socialize with white women.

I wondered why there were different rules for black and white people and Mom explained that God wanted it that way. She said that there were many verses in the Bible showing that God commands people of different colors to be kept separate here on earth and even after they go to heaven. She said the next time that Dad held Sunday church services at our house she would ask him to show me some of the verses and explain them. "In the meantime," she said, "just know we're following God's rules and they work just fine. As you get older, you'll understand them better and better."

"Yeah," Joan said mockingly, "when you git older you'll be able to understand things!" Then she kicked me. Joan took great delight in kicking me in the shin, and she was very good at doing it in a way that our parents never saw it. And I wondered why it was wrong to hit girls—especially ones as mean as my sister.

After we watched people for a couple of hours, Dad and Mom would leave Joan and me alone while they walked to a local drugstore and bought four ice cream cones for a nickel each; I always asked for the black walnut flavor and Joan asked for chocolate. They would bring back the ice cream and we would eat it in the car. The four of us would continue to sit in the car and watch the people passing by until the ice cream was gone. Then, on the way back to the farm, Dad would stop at a small grocery store, run in and buy some chili, the solid kind that looked like a reddish orange brick with solid white fat at the top. When we got home, he would fire up the wood stove in the kitchen, boil some water, chop up the bricks of chili and mix it into the water—this was the only cooking he would do. Marie would join us sometimes while we ate the chili with soda crackers crumbled in it. Thanks to the money from the AOP, we started an enjoyable family custom of going to town on Saturday evening, watching people and eating ice cream and chili.

While we remained very poor, our wealth did gradually increase and we bought a lot of things we never had before. Coal oil, the same oil we burned for lighting, had also been used as a general purpose antiseptic to put on cuts and bruises but we bought a bottle of iodine because it was supposed to work better; however, its sting was much worse. We also bought aspirin for the first time, bandages, Vick's Salve and Alka Seltzer. Soon the orange crate cabinet nailed to the kitchen wall that had held both dishes and small amounts of medicine was now filled with only medicine and lots of different kinds too. The dishes were moved to their very own orange crate.

It came as a complete surprise one day when Mom asked Dad a question in such a way that I knew they had been thinking and talking about moving. "Did you send in the papers for that guard job up in Washington?" she asked. "Yes," Dad said, "a few days ago. I expect a lot of other men did too cause the pay's so good—more than you and I make combined."

BORROWED BIBLES

They had been talking to each other in a low voice for some time whenever I was around but I thought they were just doing regular grown-up talk that kids weren't supposed to hear. Now I knew it meant we might be moving depending on how far Washington was of course and depending on whether or not Dad got the job.

"How far is Washington?" I asked Mom as soon as I could be alone with her.

"It's about as far as you can git and still be in America. It's way up North and over on the West coast. Have Mrs. West show you on the globe at school tomorrow." And I did.

Dad was offered the job and he accepted. From that time on it seemed like every minute of our lives was filled with thinking about and preparing for the move from Arkansas to Washington. And only a few days later, Marie made a major decision and announced that she wouldn't be moving with the rest of us. She took her few possessions with her—the only significant one was a cedar hope chest half filled with linens, and towels—and rented a room closer to Jacksonville. She continued to work at the AOP and was very happy to move out. She had been thinking about doing it for some time and our move to Washington just served as an impetus. Although an adult at 20 years of age, Marie had very little freedom living with us and Joan and I were too young to give her the company she needed. She was 15 years older than me and unfortunately I didn't know her very well. It made me sad, though, that she was so eager to leave home that she didn't take the time to say goodbye to Joan or me.

The prospect of making so much money made my parents excited and this led to a happy family atmosphere. On the other hand there was quite a bit of anxiety based on what living in Washington would be like. Mom had heard that it rained an awful lot "up there" and while it would be good to get away from the Arkansas hot weather, too much rain would also be hard to take. Dad kidded us by saying all that rain would make us all grow webfeet like a duck. "No," said Mom, "web feet is what they grow in Oregon but come to think of it, we'll be right across the river from Oregon so maybe we will!"

"Well, the real problem," said Dad, "is that up there they allow mixing of the races. So we're gonna have the blacks in the same bathrooms, churches, cafes and anywhere else they'll want to be. And the kids are gonna have them in school. I don't know what's gonna come of that. Bob Hendricks there at AOP moved up two years ago and he only lasted one year and moved back here. He couldn't take all that mixing. I just don't know, but on the other hand, some folks learn to get along with it too so we'll just have to see for ourselves. Meanwhile, I'll be making real good money."

Dad and Mom decided to not only sell the farm but also what little furniture we had, the two mules, the two cows, the chickens and the Chevrolet. We would take the train from Little Rock, Arkansas to a new residential development called Bagley Downs located in Vancouver, Washington right across the Columbia River from Portland, Oregon. Our new home would be close to the Vancouver shipyard where Dad would be a guard. We would take only two suitcases on the train with us and ship two trunks as freight. We were not able to find new homes for our dogs, Penny and Fanny, so we planned to leave them behind. I hoped they would stay alive until the new owner arrived to take charge of our farm and I hoped the new owner liked dogs. We would also wait a few weeks before we moved so Joan and I could finish out the school year in Lonoke. Although Mom and Dad disagreed on a lot of things, they both believed in the importance of a good education and this served as a positive driving force for our family. It was just understood that no matter what, we kids would all finish high school at least and finish as soon as possible. And the boys were encouraged to go as far beyond high school as possible, maybe even earning doctorates as my brother Bill eventually did. It was different for the girls, Marie and Joan, but they were expected to graduate from high school and perhaps go to secretarial or nursing school; however, going to college was not discussed.

Dad knew a man, Arthur, at AOP who owned a car and a pickup truck and Dad hired him to drive our belongings and us to the train station in Little Rock. When the two vehicles pulled into our farm, Dad, Arthur and the driver of the pickup placed our trunks and suitcases on the truck bed and threw a canvas over them. Mom, Joan and I climbed into the back seat of the car with me in the middle. Dad sat in the front passenger seat. We were all excited, but apprehensive, quiet and a little sad because we were leaving so many familiar things even if some were unpleasant. I leaned forward and took a last look at our farmhouse hoping I wouldn't see our dogs because that would make me even sadder. Fortunately, Penny and Fanny weren't in sight and I figured they were sleeping in the back yard like they often were at that time of day. All the same, leaving them behind was still very sad and it reminded me of leaving Charlie when the Army moved us. But at least this time the Army wouldn't destroy our farm. The new owner might take care of Penny and Fanny and this time we had sold our chickens.

Arthur started the car and headed toward the train station in Little Rock. The pickup holding all our possessions followed along behind us with the canvas, partially loose, flapping in the wind. Mom was alarmed by the flapping and shouted, "Stop! We're gonna lose everything." Arthur chuckled, "No Ma'am, it's gonna be just fine. Don't worry cause we got her tied down real good and she just naturally flaps like that."

I had heard that Little Rock was big but as we drove through the streets headed for the train station I was still surprised to see how big it really was. It was much bigger than Lonoke. There were so many people, streets, cars and buses and noise. I asked Joan if it was the biggest city in the world and she laughed and said, "Course not, just the biggest in Arkansas and it's nowhere as big as Memphis or Chicago. But speakin about the world, that's gotta be the dumbest question in the world!" She laughed and I'm sure she would've kicked me in the shin then if Mom hadn't been sitting on the other side of me and would've seen her do it.

Our train was scheduled to leave at 7:00 p.m. and we arrived at the station about three hours earlier. After our trunks and suitcases were checked in, Dad said we'd all go for a walk around Little Rock while there was good daylight and as a special treat we would get supper at a real high-class cafe. Joan and I walked behind Mom and Dad and took in all the amazing sights including the sidewalks that were so much wider than those in Lonoke. Joan said, "It must be a mile wide," and she took my hand and led me in walking a zigzag pattern using up the whole width of the sidewalk. This drew a look of severe disapproval from Mom so we stopped it. Joan was five years older than me but this was also the first time she had been to Little Rock and she was just as amazed at the sights as I was. We stopped often to look through the windows of stores selling clothes, books, furniture and all sorts of other things. Dad was impatient with us stopping so much and kept telling us, "Hurry along." There were lots of other people on the sidewalk too including farmers, soldiers and two strange women walking in the opposite direction dressed head to foot in scary black robes. I asked Joan what they were and she didn't know saying she had never seen anything like them. So, I asked Mom and she shushed me saying, "Don't talk so loud." She and Dad stopped walking and led Joan and me to the edge of the sidewalk away from everyone else where Mom told us in a low voice, "Now, those are Catholic women that they call nuns. They always travel at least two together in a pack, and they carry razor blades underneath those black robes. If you aren't a Catholic child, they'll grab you if they get the chance, put you under their robes and carry you away and make you into a Catholic. If anyone tries to stop them, they'll be cut up with those razor blades they got. Now, let's keep going." I turned around and looked apprehensively at the nuns but they had kept walking and were now quite a distance away. We seemed safe for the time being but I had learned that if I ever saw nuns again, I would have to be very careful.

"We'll eat here," Dad said. We were standing on the sidewalk outside the Pepper Pot Café and Dad said he could tell it was the kind of high-class place that we deserved on this special occasion because it had white curtains covering up the front windows. "It'll keep busy bodies from standing out here on the sidewalk and looking at us while we eat. Now, that's high-class!" When we got inside, Dad walked up to the woman standing at the front desk and said proudly and with great authority, "Table for four!" A waitress gave us each a menu and Mom told us it was OK to look at the menu but she and Dad would do the ordering for us. Dad ordered meat loaf and Mom ordered beef stew and told the waitress to bring two extra empty plates, "for the children." Joan and I were told to stay quiet and not fidget in our chairs while we waited for our food, and we did even though it seemed like a long wait. After the waitress brought our food, Mom divided it up and served Joan and me our portions. Then, we wolfed down our food so fast and so loud that some people at the other tables turned to look and they shook their heads in disgust. They probably were amazed with our table manners that were common with Arkansas country folks. We didn't use forks at all but only used our spoons most of the time. And sometimes we used spoons to push food onto our knife blade and then we'd pull the knife blade loaded with food through our mouth. Dad was so good using a knife that way that he could easily eat peas with a knife. "Well, we're not like some folks, we've had to work hard and we're hungry," Dad said to no one in particular but he purposely said it loud enough so everyone could hear—especially the people staring at us. Mom said she and Dad had a surprise and that since it was a special occasion, we could each have a piece of pie and we could choose apple or lemon. I chose lemon because I had never eaten it before but everyone else chose apple. I discovered I didn't like lemon because it was so sour and I didn't see the sense in even having dessert if it wasn't sweet.

After we ate the pie, Dad gave money to the waitress for the food and kept the change she brought back. As usual he didn't leave a tip because he didn't believe in receiving or giving charity. And he looked thoughtful and sad as he talked to us while we were still seated, "This'll be the last meal we'll have here in Arkansas and that's why I wanted it to be so good and so high-class. I've lived here all my life, about 50 long years, and I don't know what it'll be like livin somewhere else but it could be real good. We'll soon see. In a little while our train's gonna leave and we'll head north and go into the state of Missouri and then somewhere we're gonna turn west then we'll turn north and we'll keep goin until we reach Vancouver, where our new home will be. We'll be there in four days. Now, let's hurry back to the station cause it took longer here than I first thought and our train won't wait."

We hurried so we wouldn't be late just like Dad wanted; in fact we were almost running. There was less traffic on the streets than when we first arrived in Little Rock, and that made the small Army convoy, made up of three jeeps and two trucks, that passed us very conspicuous. This time I didn't have to ask any questions because Mom figured that seeing the convoy would cause me concerns. She said, "Those are our soldiers and they're probably from Camp Joe T. Robinson. It's only a few miles north of here and with the war going on soldiers are moving around every which way." And she asked me, "Do you remember Luther and the other soldiers that moved us to Steel Bridge?" I said that I did. "Well, they were from Camp Robinson and when they took over our farm, they made it part of Camp Robinson too." What she told me helped my understanding a bit but my main concern with the convoy was that it reminded me of Charlie and Charlie reminded me of

Penny and Fanny. I didn't mention that part, though, because I didn't want to cause any trouble.

The train car that we boarded had an aisle down the middle with two adjoining seats on each side of the aisle. As expected, Joan and I were told to sit together and since she was the oldest and a girl she got to choose what seat she wanted. She figured out real quick that I wanted the seat next to the window so naturally she chose that one. On the other hand, every time she had to leave her seat she had to scoot right past me and that gave me a good opportunity to punch her. Mom and Dad wanted to sit in the seats just across the aisle from me but soldiers occupied them so they had to go up three rows to sit. Every once in a while Mom would turn around to make sure we were behaving.

We were sitting in what was called a "day car" because there were no special provisions for sleeping. We were expected to sleep in our seats sitting upright but to help us sleep, the conductors turned the aisle lights down at night. Then, too, by pulling a lever on the arm of the seat and pushing backward the seat would recline into a more comfortable position. As another special treat, Dad agreed to rent a pillow for each of us for the four-day train trip.

As the train began to move out, the soldiers, and there were quite a few of them, stood up, cheered and clapped their hands. I didn't know what the commotion was about but I was happy that they seemed so happy. The soldier across the aisle from me lifted an empty beer bottle in the air and said, "I wish it was full again!" Joan whispered to me to not pay attention to him because drinking beer was a sin. There were other soldiers that were drinking beer and some were even playing cards; I knew that was a sin too.

There was still some daylight as we moved north through the outskirts of Little Rock and then through North Little Rock and then we continued north to the Missouri state line as darkness fell. I noticed that Joan had reclined her seat and was asleep and even though she pestered me a lot I missed her company and felt very lonely. I pulled the lever on the side of my seat, pushed my seat back and fell asleep too.

"Quick, I gotta go," Joan whispered in my ear as she gently shook me. It was unusual for her to be so gentle with me so I decided not to punch her as she scooted past me to get to the bathroom She had awakened me up from a sound sleep and to morning sunlight and to hunger. The soldiers across the aisle were still asleep as were most people but I could see that Mom and Dad were talking to each other so I walked up to where they were sitting. Mom greeted me and said we weren't in Arkansas anymore and wasn't it fun sleeping on the train and that Dad had bought Joan and me each a donut for breakfast. She said I could wash it down with water from the fountain by the bathroom at the end of the car. I told her Joan had gone to that very bathroom and Mom said, "Fine, you go too. Eat your donut, give this other one to Joan and drink all the water you want, but remember before you eat—wash your hands first."

After we ate our donuts, Joan and I went back to our seats and passed the time by looking out the window and playing spelling games. Ever so often a woman would walk down the aisle with a tray of food held in place by a strap around her neck. The tray had sandwiches and candy bars for sale and Dad bought us sandwiches for dinner and supper. He said that if we continued to behave properly and stay out of trouble, he would buy us a candy bar on the last day of the train ride.

I asked Mom and Dad if I could walk to the end of the train and they said yes but to not bother anyone and to stay out of other people's way. They said I would know when I came to the end of the train because the last car wouldn't have any white folks in it but would be filled with black folks. It was hard walking in the aisle when the train was going around a curve or going over rough track, but I got used to it and entered the car behind us. It was pretty much like our car with every seat taken and with soldiers making a lot of noise. The next car was like our car too but the car after that was the dining car where people with a lot of money ate. There were quite a few tables and they all had white table clothes on them and a flower in a vase that looked like silver. There was a silver looking candlestick and a silver looking coffee pot on each table too. There were two black waiters taking care of the tables and they gave me unfriendly looks as I squeezed past their serving carts in the aisle. "Children don't belong here without their parents," one of the waiters said. I hurried through the dining car and entered the car just behind it. I was greeted by a car full of black folks who looked at me with unfriendly eyes that questioned what a white kid was doing in their car. I felt threatened, turned around and walked

FROM SEGREGATION TO INTEGRATION TO SEGREGATION

as fast as I could back through the dining car and the other two cars and happily returned to my seat.

The conductor walked down the aisle and announced loudly and in an official voice, "No segregation from this point on. Any questions?" He announced it several times in our car and I could hear him announcing it again as he walked through the car behind us. "No segregation from this point on. Any questions?"

I asked Joan, "Why's he doing that?"

Joan answered, "Well, there're places where the races don't mix like in Arkansas where we lived till now—that's called segregation. Then, there're places in the country where the races can mix and we're in that part of the country now—that's called integration. What's more, we're gonna be in integration country from now on and when we git to Vancouver we're gonna live in integration. That's what the conductor meant. So, the black people that are sittin in the last car on this train can now sit anywhere there's a vacant seat. They can use any bathroom. They can sit in the same cafe, go to the same schools and churches. You understand now?"

"Well sorta and I heard Mom and Dad talk about it before we left Arkansas. But I don't see how there can even be integration if the Bible says God wants segregation."

"Well, some folks don't believe the Bible says that. Other folks say that even if the Bible does say that, the important thing is that God couldn't have said that. It's scary and I don't think integration is natural."

I thought the train ride to Vancouver would be nothing but fun but I was discouraged, saddened, and disappointed by all the sinning. I believed God and Jesus would feel even worse than I did because of all the beer drinking, card playing and integration. God had warned us, and if we made God mad with all our sinning, there was no telling what he might do to the train.

Sometimes it was hard to see out the train window because Joan blocked the view and the steam from the engine sometimes created a fog. Nevertheless, I was able to see a wide variety of scenery after we left Arkansas including rolling hills, a desert I thought would never end and canyons. At one point the train slowed way down and lots of people got out of their seats to go to a window and look out. The train was not only going real slow but it was swaying badly from side to side and there were a lot of gasps and yells from people looking out. "Look how high up we are," Joan shouted. I did look out and saw we were on a bridge and it seemed we were a mile above a river. There was no land below us just a bridge and the train slowed down almost to a stop and the swaying got worse. I was afraid the train would fall off the bridge and I figured that would be God's punishment I had been dreading. But although it did take a long time, we made it to the other side and the train picked up speed again. God had let us get by with just a warning for the time being.

Mom told us that the train was preparing to stop in Denver where we would have a four-hour wait until we continued our trip. It would be a good chance to leave the train, get some exercise and look around inside the station. I could hardly wait and I stood next to the conductor who was by the exit door getting ready to open it. He said the obvious, "Can't wait to get off, eh boy? Well, don't outrun your parents and get back here and board on time because we won't wait for you." With that, he opened the door and I hurried down the train steps and jumped to the platform of the Denver, Colorado train station. I was the first passenger off the train.

The rest of the family soon joined me and we walked around the inside of the station and marveled how much larger it was than the station in Little Rock. We looked at a large newsstand that had all kinds of newspapers and magazines for sale and Dad decided to buy a Denver newspaper to find out what was going on with the war. He said that after he and Mom finished reading it, he would give the funny papers to Joan and me to read. Joan asked to buy a romance magazine like the kind that Marie read but Mom said, "No, I won't let you read that trashy stuff."

Joan pouted and then said, "But Marie was allowed to read them."

Mom replied, "Well, Marie's grown-up, a whole ten years older than you and she can read what she wants. Besides she bought those trashy magazines with her own money. When you get to be grown-up, you can spend your own money on trashy stuff if you want to."

Dad decided that we should have a hot meal before we boarded our train again because he was tired of just eating cold sandwiches he bought from the woman with the tray. He warned us, though, to not expect anything as high-class as the meal we had at the Pepper Pot in Little Rock. We walked over to a stand that sold hamburgers and hot dogs and Dad ordered four hot dogs and four Cokes. Dad, Joan and I sat on barstools while we ate ours but Mom stood next to Dad to eat hers. She said it was a lot more ladylike to stand up and eat than sit on a barstool. I noticed that there were a couple of black folks sitting on the stools too and even though I had been warned about integration, it was an unsettling experience. I was also worried about drinking Coke because Dad had always said it was a sin and I didn't understand why he ordered them—so I asked him.

Dad said, "I ordered them cause they don't have any Royal Crowns here. But there's a war goin on and we have an emergency so God's gonna cut us slack." I was glad God did that because I thought Coke tasted a whole lot better than Royal Crown even though there wasn't as much in the bottle. Joan thought so too and she had planned to sneak a Coke someday to see what they were like. Now she wouldn't have to.

We boarded our train and once again we were the last four passengers to be seated. Most of the passengers we started out with in Little Rock had left the train for good and Mom and Dad were now seated across the aisle from me. The soldier that had sat across from me and drank all that beer got off the train at Denver, and most of the other soldiers got off too.

I noticed that some of the new passengers that boarded in Denver were black folks sitting in what until recently was a segregated, all white car. The integrated seating made us uneasy. It was new to our family because we had lived all our lives in segregation. I wondered if the black folks noticed our uneasiness and were uneasy too.

If I hadn't already been on the train for so long, I'm sure that the last part of the trip from Denver to Vancouver would've been exciting and very interesting. We did travel through a magnificent part of the United States with gorgeous mountains, valleys and rivers. I was very tired of the train ride, though, and eager to be settled again. Even though it would mean putting up with integration, I looked forward to a new home, to sleeping in a real bed, and eating something besides cold sandwiches bought from the woman with the tray. And Dad did buy Joan and me a candy bar from that woman with the tray on the last day of our trip as he had promised.

"You said you wanted to go to Bagley Downs and here we are!" Those were the welcome words from the shuttle driver who drove us from the Vancouver train station to our new home.

Bagley Downs was a new, government sponsored housing development constructed for the massive influx of civilian defense workers into the Vancouver area. Shortly after the attack on Pearl Harbor, the federal government contracted with industrialist Henry J. Kaiser to build and operate two major shipyards in the Portland, Oregon-Vancouver, Washington area namely, Vancouver Ship, and Oregon Ship. They joined the Swan Island shipyard already in existence. Operating these three shipyards had a major impact on employment in the area; the largest payroll of 1,100 workers in 1940 grew to over 97,000 workers by the end of 1943, the year that our family moved to Vancouver. To build and maintain this labor force was a challenge to Henry Kaiser as he acknowledged in his famous statement, "If they know one end of a monkey wrench from the other, we'll take them as helpers. If they don't, we'll label each end."

Bagley Downs Housing Development, Vancouver, Washington, January 1944. [Courtesy of: Files/The Columbian]

FROM SEGREGATION TO INTEGRATION TO SEGREGATION

The shipyards operated seven days a week, 24 hours a day and produced over 700 navy ships by the end of World War II. To accommodate this massive population growth, a new federal entity, The Vancouver Housing Authority (VHA), was formed to build and manage six major housing developments: Fruit Valley, Burton Homes, Fourth Plain Village, Ogden Meadows, McLoughlin Heights, and Bagley Downs with 2,100 apartment houses where we moved to. The prefabricated apartments were meant to be only temporary and they were only rented—none were sold. The first Bagley Downs units that were rented had an electric refrigerator and electric stoves but the later units, like ours, were equipped with an icebox and coal burning stoves. While the units were luxurious compared to the Arkansas shacks we had lived in, the World War II Bagley Downs development was widely known as the "ghetto of Vancouver" to much of the surrounding populace.

The sky was featureless, gray and dropped to the ground much like fog. And it was misting, then raining, and then misting again, changing every few minutes. Dampness passed through the shuttle, through our clothes, and came to rest in our lungs. A lot of newcomers found the Vancouver mist, rain, dampness and featureless skies hard to take and some never did learn to take it. They might have tolerated it if it had only lasted a few days but it could last for months and that sometimes led to dark, bone-deep depression. After a few months, some would pack up and go back; it didn't matter to where because they felt that, "anyplace is better than this." But those that could take it, and some even liked it, were treated to gorgeous spring and summer days with lush foliage and a perfect sky everywhere.

Dad said to the shuttle driver, "This weather is mighty different than the kind we had in Arkansas where we just left." The driver answered, "I bet it is! You better get used to it too because we've got lots of weather like this. And in the rainy season from late September through March we can go for lots of days without seeing the sun. Well, we've only got a few more blocks to go and then you and your family will be at your new home." I didn't like what the driver had to say about the weather plus he was hard to understand because of his strange accent.

The drive through Bagley Downs to our new home was very confusing. The 2,100 apartment houses looked the same and there was row after row of them. I figured it would take a long time to understand how to go anywhere without getting lost. And there were no trees, just a few bushes here and there and very little grass. There were a few kids playing in the streets; some were riding bikes and they scurried to the side of the street to let our shuttle pass by. And on one street I noticed something I had never seen before—black and white kids playing some kind of ball game together.

We stopped at a small grocery store only a few blocks from our home that had been made to look like an apartment house so it would blend in. Mom opened up her purse and handed Dad a list saying, "Get as many of these groceries as you can cause this will be our food stuff until we get settled." The rest of us waited in the shuttle while Dad bought the groceries. It didn't take him long to come out of the store holding two large bags that he passed to me and Joan. Mom saw that holding the bags was uncomfortable but she said it wouldn't be for long because we were so close to our new home that we could even walk to it if we had to. I looked into the bags and saw cans of sardines, bricks of chili, soda crackers, peanut butter, a bottle of aspirin and a jar of Vick's salve.

"Here we are," the driver said. He helped Dad carry the suitcases and groceries into the house, told us goodbye and wished us luck. He returned to the shuttle and drove off. Our trip from Arkansas had sort of ended before but now that the shuttle driver had left and we were alone, it had definitely ended and with finality.

Our new home had three bedrooms and someone from the VHA had left two cots in the largest bedroom and one cot in the other two. There was also a stack of blankets and some pillows in one of the bedrooms. The living room had a folding table, folding chairs and a coal-burning stove. There was a small bin next to the stove that contained coal and kindling wood. There was another coal-burning stove in the kitchen as well as an icebox. The last room in the house, the bathroom, was the best room of all. Not only was there running water and a toilet like we had at the Lonoke School but there was also a shower. This was the first house our family had with electricity and running water although we had seen these features in public places but none of us had ever taken a shower. When we needed a bath, we filled up a washtub in our backyard, heated the water with a wood fire and stepped in. We took a bath about every two months sometimes more often in the summertime. Mom was standing behind me as I was looking and said, "Yes, that's a shower and I expect you to use it at least once a week. And start before you go to bed tonight cause you smell pretty bad."

Joan and I decided to investigate the backyard while there was still some daylight but as soon as we opened the back door, we discovered there wasn't much to investigate. It was only a few feet from our back door to an alley. On the other side of the alley there was an apartment identical to ours. To our left, there was an apartment identical to ours and to our right there was an apartment identical to ours. In fact, wherever we looked in Bagley Downs there were identical apartment houses. There was almost no room to play in the alley but there were large coal bins located ever so often full of coal to be shared by the apartments. We had never seen coal before so we walked to the nearest bin and looked at it closely and felt it. The weather was still alternating between a mist and rain turning the surface of the coal into an ink-like slush, which gave me the idea of smearing some on Joan's face. She squealed but then rubbed some on my face and we both started laughing and decided to paint our faces like Indians. We thought our Indian make-up was funny and hurried back inside the house to show Mom and Dad. We thought they might laugh about our make-up too but they became very angry and took turns shouting at us. Dad shouted the angriest and loudest but Mom shouted the longest, "Your Dad and I are dog tired and worn out! It's cold and we're wet and hungry and trying to get a new place goin and you kids have to misbehave like that! And you put all that coal stuff on you on purpose. I'm ashamed of you two! Well, now you're gonna take your showers early, then you're gonna have some supper and then you're gonna go to bed early! Joan, you first!" Mom didn't shout like that unless she was dead serious.

Dad had started a fire in the living room stove and we sat around it and ate a cold supper of crackers and sardines from flat, wind-up cans washed down with water. Mom said she was sorry that we had to eat cold food from a can but she would soon be rested enough to start cooking hot meals. In the meantime, we enjoyed the cold sardines more than the cold sandwiches we bought on the train.

Joan and I went to our bedrooms. As expected, she had chosen the best one. I crawled on to my cot and relished the good feeling of lying down rather than sitting in a train car.

It took a few months but our apartment gradually reached a state that was more or less normal by our standards. Dad settled into his job as a guard at the shipyard, routinely caught the bus to and from work, and was pleased with the paycheck he brought home every week. Mom stayed home and tended full time to the house and yard. Our two trunks arrived with several dents on the outside but none of the possessions inside were damaged. Mom and Dad bought some used furniture for every room in the house including several floor lamps that made it easy to read at night for the first time in our lives. We bought a radio that was powered by electricity so we had a form of entertainment without worrying about battery life. An iceman delivered ice on a regular schedule and we were able to keep leftover food that otherwise would have spoiled. We learned to bring in the right amount of coal so we would have plenty to cook and heat with. And each of us learned how to find our way to and from the local grocery store even though the look-alike apartments were still confusing.

Joan and I walked two blocks to catch the bus to Arnada School. A lot of kids lived in Bagley Downs so there were lots of school buses and bus routes. We would wait with about 20 other kids, and sometimes a few guardian parents, to catch our particular bus. Unlike the ride to the Lonoke School where Joan and I were the outsiders and harassed a lot because of that and because of our whitewashed house, there were no insider or outsider kids at Bagley Downs. We were all new residents and social structures hadn't been formed yet. So when we waited for the bus, there was almost no talking only an awkward silence. The white kids who were in the majority waited in one group and the four black kids in another. When we boarded the bus, the black kids went to the back of the bus and the rest of us spread out in the front. We separated into two groups not because we were required to but because it seemed natural and felt comfortable.

During my first day at Arnada School, I waited to see my new teacher, Miss Jordan, alone so I could talk to her in private. I wanted to know if white and black kids really would have to use the same bathrooms and playgrounds. After experiencing the train ride from

Arkansas and hearing my parent's concern about integration, I was pretty sure that I knew the answer but I wanted to make sure I was following the rules. I also wanted to know if there were any loopholes in the rules. She replied, "I bet from the way you talk you used to live in Oklahoma or Arkansas and rules are different down there, I know. But here, blacks and whites do use the same bathrooms and there's only one playground and both blacks and whites use it." She gave me a big smile and added, "It's just fine so don't worry. You'll get used to it and find out it really doesn't matter."

I argued, "But the Bible says the races shouldn't mix and they don't even mix in heaven!"

Miss Jordan replied, "Most all preachers of all churches don't believe the Bible says that. Most preachers believe that God and Jesus want everyone to be treated equal. Nobody is forcing races to mix; we just want everyone to have the right to do it if they choose and to have equal rights. Now, go outside to the playground. It's a nice day and you need to start playing with your classmates. You'll be happier when you do."

I went to the playground after lunch and was amazed at its enormous size. It was very well designed to hold all the kids from the first through the eighth grade that shared it. There were several swing sets, seesaws and lots of empty space where kids could just run or invent their own games. Three adults were supervising several types of games and some students were just sitting around picnic-type tables and talking. And just like on the bus, the black kids and white kids formed their own separate groups for the most part. Others, including me, were standing alone at the edge of the playground because we didn't want to talk to anyone else or didn't know how to do it. I was looking for Joan to talk with. Ordinarily, she would be one of the last people I would want to talk to but after experiencing the new school with strange rules, it would be a relief. I saw her sitting at a table talking with two black girls and I walked over to her.

Joan introduced me as her little brother and the two girls apparently feeling uncomfortable around a white boy walked away immediately and joined a group of black kids.

"I don't like this school," I said to Joan. "How about you?"

BORROWED BIBLES

"Well, I've had a good time. My teachers are good and said interesting things and the kids are real friendly—much friendlier than those kids at the Lonoke School. Why don't you like it?"

"My teacher told me that some people think that what the Bible says is wrong! How could it be wrong? And besides you I haven't had anyone to talk with. And how come you were talkin to those two black girls all friendly like? Why aren't you with your own kind?"

"Well, this morning my teacher asked everyone in the room to tell where we lived last year and almost everyone had lived in another state. There were at least five other kids that had lived in Arkansas and I found that real interesting. Those two black girls, named Jane and Jennifer, are twins and it's so strange but they lived in Carlisle—and that's just a skip and a jump down the road from Lonoke! So after class it seems we were kinda drawn to each other cause they've been lonely up here and down in Arkansas we were neighbors. So we just sat down here and began to talk about things. One of the things they did, just like us, was to go to Lonoke on Saturday afternoon to look at people, walk down the street and buy ice cream cones. They could have been some of the very black folks we were watchin when we were settin in our car. Isn't that interesting?"

"I don't remember seeing black twin girls." I said. I was mad because she was happy with our new school and I wasn't. "Anyway," I continued, "You shoulda been with your own kind. We can't help being on the same bus and in the same school but we gotta remember what Dad and Mom and the Bible says about mixing races."

"What I did wasn't mixin; it was just talkin. And almost everyone up here looks at the Bible in a different way than we were taught. Besides it was interesting talkin to them and I don't see how that could hurt anything."

"Well, we gotta get a new preacher fast and I guess we will as soon as Dad finds a good church. I wanta find out what's right once and for all. I don't understand why some preachers say one thing about the Bible and other preachers say something different. I wanta sit down with a new preacher and understand it. And you know what?"

"No," Joan said. "Tell me."

"I'm gonna study and learn how to be a preacher when I grow up. That way I can figure out what God and Jesus wants all by myself without having to ask anyone."

Joan chuckled, "You've gotta long way to go before you can be a preacher. Anyway, the bell just rang so we need to get back to classes."

We didn't own a car while we lived in Bagley Downs so we didn't do any people watching on Saturday afternoon like we did at Lonoke. We continued our tradition, however, of sitting around the kitchen table on Saturday evening and sometimes eating ice cream and chili as a special treat. It was not easy to find brick chili so we got used to eating chili that came in a can. And for some reason black walnut ice cream was almost impossible to find so we got by with chocolate and vanilla. During one of our Saturday events, Dad said that he had been checking out a lot of preachers in the area and didn't like any of them because they were too Yankeefied. He said it was more dangerous to go to one of those watered-down churches than to not go at all. "The Bible warns against false prophets and those preachers are just that. And it wouldn't surprise me to find the anti-Christ living around here. With the world war going on and all the sinnin going on, it would be a perfect time for him to come. So what I'm gonna do is teach you kids religion myself. Now, I'm not someone that went through preacher's school but I do know the Bible and I know how real preachers preach. So, on Sunday mornings we're gonna go to the living room and I'm gonna lead us in old-time church services done the right way. Some day, we might invite neighbors to join us."

Mom said, "Well, OK, but let's keep lookin for the right kind of church too." And she hinted that she was getting tired of staying home all the time and with the kids in school she didn't see why she would have to. And, besides, having extra money would be nice.

The new home, new school and all the new rules weren't the only events causing trauma and nervousness in our lives. Daily newspaper articles and radio programs were providing frightening information about World War II. Since the massive attack on Pearl Harbor by the Japanese and their seemingly unstoppable march across the Pacific, there were worries about an invasion of our west coast and perhaps being totally conquered. And there were constant rumors about Japanese submarines shelling cities as well as Japanese firebomb balloons setting forest fires in Oregon and Washington—and some of the firebomb rumors were true. The Vancouver-Portland area was an enticing military target with three major shipyards, a major aluminum plant and several large dams nearby so as a defensive measure blackout strategies were employed. Many of the buildings had their windows painted black to keep light from being seen by enemy aircraft.

Some residents of Chinese origin wore a sign on their back when they went out in public that read, "I am Chinese." Several had been mistaken for Japanese and treated badly and in some cases physically abused as retaliation for the Pearl Harbor attack. The Chinese residents were eager to explain that China and the United States had Japan as a common enemy.

Joan and I volunteered for the "Boy Commandos," a civil defense group for Bagley Downs kids where we learned how to dive for cover when the commander blew his whistle and how to identify airplanes. As a reward for joining the group, we were given a password to see a free movie at a participating theater if we whispered the password in the usher's ear. The first movie I saw was, *Lifeboat*, and I saw it with Joan. I still have vivid memories of the stark set, and the actor, William Bendix, partly because of his unusual voice and partly because I listened to him a few years later on the old radio show, *The Life of Riley*. And I have very special memories of the lead actress, Tallulah Bankhead, because of her husky voice and unusual name. (Some thirty years after first seeing *Lifeboat*, I learned through my genealogical research that Tallulah is a fifth cousin. She is the most famous, as well as the most infamous, relative I have discovered in forty years of research.)

Another thing that kids did during World War II to help the war effort was to buy War Savings Stamps (WSS) that were sold in two denominations: $0.25 and $0.10. When the value of the stamps totaled $18.75, they could be exchanged for a War Bond that could be cashed ten years later for $25.00. We had a class project at Arnada School to save enough stamps to buy a jeep for the Army. This took almost the whole school year but we did it. And it was a proud day when an Army corporal drove "our" jeep to our school to show us the jeep we had bought and to thank us. Then, he took three of us at a time for a short ride and continued the rides until our entire class and Miss Jordan had been driven.

FROM SEGREGATION TO INTEGRATION TO SEGREGATION

The war continued to have very personal connections to our family. In addition to Dad employed as a guard at the shipyard, my brother J.C. was in the Army Air Force and stationed in England and my brother Bill was in the Coast Guard aboard a Destroyer Escort stationed primarily in Alaska. We proudly displayed a service flag, known as a "son in the service flag" in our front window with two blue stars, one for J.C. and one for Bill. If a service member was killed, the blue star would be replaced with a gold one and there were quite a few gold stars on display in the Bagley Downs area. When Mom read about bombing raids over Europe or battles in the Pacific, she would often get nosebleeds from worrying that one of her sons had been killed. Her nosebleeds were made worse by uncontrolled high blood pressure and could last several hours. They were very scary to see.

Joan and I finished the school year at Arnada School with no major problems. The teachers were very impressive and challenged me much more than I had been in Arkansas. Miss Jordan in particular had a way about her of teaching something extra and I enjoyed the way she went beyond the books and taught us extra things about science and history. And I wasn't aware of it at the time, but she encouraged us to look at things from different points of view especially when it came to politics, race, religion and other controversial subjects. She was the first person I had met that took a "devil's advocate" approach when teaching and that was very helpful, although frustrating at times. And the mixing of the races turned out not to be as big a problem as I feared. There were times on the playground when black kids would join us as we played prison ball or volleyball and it didn't make any difference. When the game was finished, the black kids would usually rejoin black groups but that was understandable. We white kids usually did the same thing because it was the most comfortable thing to do.

We enjoyed Arnada School for the most part but we attended it for only one year because our parents decided to move across the bridge to Portland, Oregon when school was out. There were several reasons for the move. Mom and Dad had become increasingly tired of living in the government designed, built and managed Bagley Downs housing project where all the apartment houses looked alike. They liked the electricity, running water and low rent but wanted a "real" neighborhood and a house with a big yard with trees. They had visited

Portland many times to do shopping and saw several neighborhoods that impressed them. In addition, Mom satisfied her longing to work again and found a job at Sears Roebuck in Portland as a lingerie sales woman. Sears paid her very well and she accumulated stock that was purchased through a generous employee stock purchase plan. And, very importantly, they wanted to own a home, not just rent one. Dad was eager to leave Bagley Downs for other reasons too and threatened to move back to Arkansas instead of moving to Portland. He was tired of living among all the "foreigners" and the preachers that were false prophets and while he reluctantly accepted integration on an emergency basis, he said he would move back with "his kind of people" someday and lead a Christian life again. He agreed, though, to move to Portland for the "time being."

We first moved to Holgate Avenue into a house with only two bedrooms, I shared one with Mom and Dad and Joan had one by herself. Holgate had a big yard, several big trees and vacant lots near-by that were fun to explore and reminded me of exploring our farm in Arkansas. We didn't live very long at Holgate, however, but moved a few blocks away to 5432 SE Lafayette Street into a two-story house with four bedrooms, a big yard and several trees. It was also very close to Foster Road and Powell Boulevard, major Portland streets that had all types of stores we could walk to. A most important reason for moving to this much larger house, was that Mom and Dad had a vision of having all five of us kids living together, something that had only occurred for a short period of time so far. Marie knew that when the war ended there would no longer be employment at the Arkansas Ordnance Plant and she hinted that she would then like to leave Arkansas and come to live with us. Mom and Dad hoped that J.C. and Bill would also "come home" and live with the rest of us when the war ended. Then, with all five kids at home, the four bedrooms would be put to good use.

After moving to Portland, Joan and I enrolled in the Creston School located within easy walking distance to our home on Lafayette Street. It was a large three-story building constructed mostly of wood in 1907. Joan was in the seventh grade and I was in the third grade. My teacher, Mrs. Maxwell, gave the appearance of not being very friendly; in fact she had something of a "drill sergeant" personality but she was very dedicated and competent. And her drill sergeant skills were put to good use. I had never been in a fire drill before but the Creston School practiced them regularly and vigorously. There was a special alarm that would sound and Mrs. Maxwell would give the order, "Stand up!" After we stood by our desk, she would shout, "Now walk!" We had been told at the beginning of the school year the order we were to walk in and also told to not waste time getting any of our possessions; we were to leave our books, lunch, coats and anything else we might have behind. We marched out of our classroom, down the stairs, out the entrance doors and on to the playground. We were instructed not to look back for any reason but to keep walking to the far side of the playground where each class had a pre-assigned space to stand. We were to keep standing in this space facing away from the school until we were told it was OK to turn around. All the time we were marching, Mrs. Maxwell walked up and down beside our column making sure we were following orders exactly and taking the drill seriously. Once, during a drill I did turn around and looked back at the schoolhouse as we were marching across the playground. Mrs. Maxwell happened to be walking close to me and she grabbed my head, roughly turned it around and shouted loudly, "No looking! Now walk!" I continued to walk to our pre-assigned space but I was shaken by Mrs. Maxwell's angry behavior. After the drill was over, she took me aside and gave me an angry lecture on how irresponsible I had been, how I had put myself in danger, and how I had put my classmates in danger. Then she sent me to the principal's office. Not only did he repeat what Mrs. Maxwell had said but he also added some words of his own and punctuated his lecture by pounding his fist on the desk. That still wasn't the end of my punishment; the next day, Mrs. Maxwell reviewed the performance of our fire drill with the class and said that we had flunked and that it was my fault. I was humiliated but I learned not to look back no matter what although I wasn't sure why the rule was there in the first place.

BORROWED BIBLES

Creston School, 1930s, Before The Fire [Courtesy of Shirley Souders]

Weeks later, the fire alarm sounded again and we started our drill as usual. I made extra sure that I didn't look back when we entered the playground but kept walking to our pre-assigned space. I stood in place looking away from the schoolhouse until Mrs. Maxwell shouted, "OK, you can turn around now." We did, and saw a terrible and scary sight. Smoke was billowing from several windows and red-orange flames were breaking through several places along the wooden sides and the roof of the school. I was so scared that it took me a while to realize how cold I was. The Creston School fire had started on a cold Monday, December 11, 1944, made more miserable by a drizzle heavy enough to dampen my hair. Ordinarily in weather like that, I would have worn a cap and heavy jacket but we weren't allowed to bring anything with us on fire drills so my new jacket and cap were still in our classroom closet being turned into ashes by the fire. My parents had just bought the jacket and I heard them talking about how expensive it was. We were much better off than when we left Arkansas but there was still no money to spare so I dreaded telling them what happened to my jacket.

FROM SEGREGATION TO INTEGRATION TO SEGREGATION

Creston Fire, Monday Morning, December 11, 1944
[Oregon Historical Society, #bb 008878]

I was worried about Joan too but I looked across the playground and saw that all the classes were in their pre-assigned spaces and safe. I realized that Joan must have lost her new coat in the fire too and that she was probably as worried about telling our parents about her coat burning up as I was.

77

BORROWED BIBLES

It was a perfect evacuation and fortunately so because the Creston School fire was a major disaster that resulted in the total destruction of the school. Thanks to the far-sighted school administrators and the excellent drills that they conducted, all the 400 students as well as all the staff were evacuated without a single injury and the vital school records were saved too. And the "don't turn around and look" policy that was strictly enforced could have contributed to the success. It could not have been known how the first through eighth grade students would react if they saw their school and possessions being destroyed by fire. The policy of marching to a safe distance before looking back was enacted to avoid massive panic. It worked.

Since the school was totally destroyed, we were sent home early and told to stay at home until we were contacted about what to do. After about a week at home, we were transferred to the Marysville School where I finished the third and fourth grades. Joan finished the eighth grade at Marysville and then attended Franklin High School where she finished the ninth grade.

Mom and Dad were not upset about the loss of our coats and they were genuinely relieved that we escaped the fire without being injured. When the school administrators saw how bad the fire was, they traveled to where there were working phones and called as many parents as they could. In addition some Portland radio stations made emergency announcements about the fire. As a result of an aggressive communication campaign, both Mom and Dad, who were at work, quickly learned of the disaster and they came home early too. Joan and I got a tearful hug from Mom and a big smile from Dad. He told us not to worry about our coats and that he would buy us new ones in the next few days. That evening we sat around the table and ate ice cream and chili; we had never done that before except on Saturday evenings.

Dad held to the belief that it was better for me not to go to church services than to go to services conducted by a false prophet but he and Mom did want me to go to Sunday school. So they checked out all those within walking distance and gave their approval to a Baptist Sunday school three blocks away. I went almost every week and enjoyed listening to our teacher, Mrs. Babcock. She had us kids, about nine of us, sit in a circle and she loaned us special magazines with illustrated stories taken from the Bible. The artwork and colors in the magazines were magnificent and helped the stories come alive as she read to us. I especially enjoyed the magazine that had the illustrated story of Noah's Ark. I saw the animals marching up a ramp into the Ark and learned how some looked that I had never heard of before. And the storm with the lightening bolts striking all around the Ark was enjoyable in a frightening sort of way. But the most important and happy lesson that Mrs. Babcock taught us was that Jesus loved everyone, especially children. She read from Mark about Jesus taking children in his arms and blessing them. And she read from Matthew about Jesus telling his disciples they would have to become like children to enter the kingdom of heaven. As she talked about Jesus' love for children she gave us each a special present—a picture of Jesus holding a child in his arms. She wanted us to always remember that no matter how many problems we had, we could turn to Him for comfort. And no matter if we lost every friend we had here on earth, we would always have a friend in Jesus who was in heaven. Then, Mrs. Babcock emphasized the lesson by leading us in the song, *What a Friend We have in Jesus*. I remembered some of the lyrics for a long time, "In His arms He'll take and shield thee; Thou wilt find a solace there." And there were times when I was overpowered by problems, that I did find comfort in knowing no matter how bad things got, Jesus was my friend.

Dad performed Sunday church services less and less often. This wasn't because of lack of interest on his part but because he became discouraged. Actually, he believed that the sinning was getting worse, that Portland was being overrun by foreigners and that all the local preachers were false prophets. One reason he had turned more pessimistic was due to his new job as a security officer in a Portland hotel. He got this job when the shipyard he worked for reduced its work force after the war was won and eliminated his job as a security guard. But he wasn't prepared for the number of disturbances in the hotel that he was called on to control. Moreover, he was sure that there were acts of prostitution that took place in some of the rooms. He finally came to the conclusion that no matter how hard he tried, there were too many forces aligned against him and that the only way for us to lead good Christian lives was to move back to Arkansas and be among our kind. He and Mom argued so often about moving back that their arguments became a virtual ritual:

"We're gonna move," he would declare. "This isn't a fittin life for the kids or me either. Everywhere you look there's drinkin, and dancin. What's more there's lots of loose women selling their bodies like no body's business. I haven't found a single preacher up here worth his salt—not one! And the weather isn't fit for a human being—it's barely fit for a duck! I almost died from pneumonia and its gotta be bad for the kids."

Mom would respond, "Well, if you leave, you'll leave without me and the kids will stay here too. We've got good jobs, a good house and we never had it nearly this good in Arkansas. And as for the weather, have you forgotten about the hot, sweaty days and nights and the sunstroke? Have you forgotten about the snakes, flies, mosquitoes, and chiggers? There was plenty of sinnin going on down there too and the kids are turning out just real fine. No sir! You can't give me Arkansas! We've come too far."

Usually, they would continue to disagree and their statements would get shorter and shorter but louder and louder. Eventually, they would be shouting at each other. Sometimes it would get violent as Dad would lose his patience and hit Mom but she would fight back. Dad was always the winner of these physical fights and that isn't surprising since at six foot three he was almost a foot taller than she was and weighed about 100 pounds more. After these fights, they wouldn't talk to each other for a few days but then they always made up; however, Dad didn't change his mind about going back to Arkansas. And he started to prepare for the move by subscribing to a newspaper containing advertisements for Arkansas farms for sale and to another newspaper containing advertisements for Arkansas schoolteachers.

Mom and Dad got their wish about having all five of their kids living with them in Portland. Marie was the first to move in with us. As she predicted, her job of assembling bomb parts in the Arkansas Ordnance Plant came to an end and instead of looking for another job in Arkansas she wanted to see what living in Oregon would be like. She took a train that traveled over the same route that we had used to move from Arkansas. When she arrived at the Portland train station, she took a cab to our house carrying two suitcases. Later her cedar hope chest arrived, now completely filled and, surprisingly, not damaged at all. She and Joan shared a bedroom at the back of the house that was the quietest and had the best view. When she moved back with us, Marie was 24 and Joan was 14. Marie quickly got a job with Mom's help at Sears Roebuck as a sales clerk and settled into her new life with very little difficulty.

J.C. received an honorable discharge from the Army Air Force at the age of 26 and moved into the remaining vacant bedroom. For a few days he enjoyed not working but soon became very bored and so he took a clerical position in downtown Portland. It didn't take him long to take a severe dislike to his job and to civilian life in general.

Bill was the last of the five children to move in after receiving an honorable discharge from the Coast Guard. He was given a choice of sharing a bedroom with J.C. or me and chose to room with J.C. figuring that he would have a lot more in common with another adult than with me, a nine-year-old kid. Bill had great mechanical aptitude, enjoyed fixing anything mechanical, and got a job in a service station on Foster Road within easy walking distance of our house. He became the station's mechanic at 21 years of age.

J.C. and Bill rapidly developed a great relationship. They were young, single and due to saving money while in the military, they had quite a bit to spend and for a while no job responsibilities. They took a bus to downtown Portland almost every evening to drink, go to nightclubs and to just generally have a good time. They realized that their behavior was against the rules of their upbringing and they openly admitted with self deprecating humor and sarcasm that they were going to the dogs. And they formally acknowledged their behavior by referring to themselves as the "bow-wow brothers." But they were very careful to never bring or drink alcohol inside the house or to come home intoxicated.

Bill had wanted a car ever since he was a boy and his job as a mechanic brought him into contact with many that interested him. He came close to buying one of the most beautiful cars I had ever seen—a raven black, 1934, Pierce Arrow sedan. The owner let Bill try it out for a few hours and he brought it by our house to show it off. It had distinctive elongated headlights that Mom said were a "mile long" and a powerful sounding but extremely smooth engine. After a lot of soul searching, however, he decided not to buy it because the Pierce Arrow Corporation had gone bankrupt a few years before and though he was a good mechanic, Bill worried about finding parts. But a short time after turning down the Pierce Arrow, he bought a dark blue, 1938, DeSoto four-door sedan. It had a hood ornament in the image of Hernando de Soto that helped make it a very striking car and Bill especially liked the engine that he thought was extremely well designed. The DeSoto gave Bill a lot of flexibility with his travels so he and J.C. journeyed together more than ever and even took a few extended trips around Oregon and Washington. Once, as a special treat, Bill drove Mom, Joan and me over to the Pacific ocean, about 90 miles west of Portland. It was the first time I had seen an ocean and I was immediately mesmerized by its beauty, size, and sound. I had never before felt such awe—an awe mixed with tranquility. The ocean trip was a spiritual experience that whispered to me that I was home. And from that day, a visit to the ocean has always brought back the same profound spiritual experience.

Bill kept tinkering with the DeSoto's engine to make it even better and he finally decided to pull the engine out, take it completely apart and improve it part by part. Our driveway at Lafayette Street was about 30 yards long and soon he had the car parked at the far end with parts of the engine reaching from the car almost out to the sidewalk. And he did go over it part by part, replaced some of them and balanced others. It took a long time to do this and Bill developed a routine where he would walk to his job at the service station during the day and at night he would work on the DeSoto. When he was outside working, Mom would hold a flashlight for him and sometimes I would take him a glass of water or a wrench. Finally, he finished rebuilding and started it up. His workmanship paid off—the engine was more powerful and noticeably much smoother. But there was a mysterious result of his rebuilding project as well. There was a part left over; Bill didn't know where it belonged and it was never put back! The engine ran fine without it but where that part actually belonged has remained one of our family mysteries.

There were some happy times as a result of our seven family members living in the same house. Christmas 1945 was a sensational success but, sadly, a success never to be repeated. On Christmas day, everyone was happy and in a festive mood. The happy feelings actually began a few days before when Mom, Marie and Joan started to put up decorations and prepare the Christmas supper. (We still referred to the evening meal as "supper"; the noon meal as "dinner" and "lunch" was what you carried in a lunch box.) When Marie had been living alone in Arkansas, she had been invited to a large Christmas day celebration and had enjoyed it so much that she vowed to plan a celebration herself one day. Fortunately, Mom and Joan enthusiastically worked with her to implement our Christmas event. We put on our best clothes as soon as we got out of bed Christmas morning and wore them the rest of the day; J.C. turned the radio on to Christmas music and we had festive background music until we went to bed that night. There were decorations on the walls and several strings of lights on our tree, our first Christmas tree and lights ever, including some remarkable bubble lights. There was a big stack of presents under the tree and for the first time there was more than one present for everyone and each one was nicely wrapped. In the early afternoon we unwrapped our presents and spent the next few hours enjoying them. Bill and J.C. exchanged Christmas cards for the first time in their lives and they thought it was funny that each of them had coincidentally signed their cards, "From your bow-wow brother." I heard some kids playing with their new presents in the street and normally I would have joined them but I stayed inside to enjoy our unusual happy family time. In the early evening, we had a large supper with ham and turkey with dressing; two kinds of potatoes; several vegetables and three kinds of pies. After supper, Dad continued his tradition of opening a coconut but on the evening of our 1945 Christmas he opened three instead of just one. The last thing we did that evening was to drink coconut milk together and sit around the living room while the adults had a contest to see who could tell the tallest yarn, something most Arkansas natives are very good at. Bill won the contest.

We were constantly getting on each other's nerves, however, and this overshadowed the rare happy times. It was troublesome to share the single bathroom with seven people and a challenge to keep the house quiet enough for Mom and Dad. More significantly, our home became the stage for some profound conflicts that had a long-term, destructive effect on our family. I wasn't aware until J.C. moved in that he and Marie had developed a life-long antagonistic relationship that bordered on hatred. They were constantly quarreling and their quarrels were loud and sometimes violent with Marie often throwing things at him. One time their argument became more violent than usual and grew to the point where J. C. threw Marie across his lap and spanked her. It wasn't a playful spanking either and J.C. kept at it with all the strength he had for a long time. Marie tried to escape but couldn't and this brought her to tears not only because of pain but also because she was humiliated. After the spanking, they didn't speak to each other and Marie vowed to move out. A few days later, a small truck pulled up in front of our house, two men got out and moved Marie's belongings into it. She got in too and the truck drove away. We didn't hear anything from her until she sent a letter to Mom and Dad announcing that she had married Kenneth Balhiser on March 2, 1946. No one in our family had been invited to the wedding.

J.C. had an antagonistic relationship with Dad also. As a male and the oldest child, he was the second "man of the house" and that inherently led to a rivalry. Then, there was also an on-going conflict because he was mother's best friend and confidant, and always took her side when she argued with Dad. Soon after J.C.'s violent argument with Marie, Mom and Dad had a similar violent argument about moving back to Arkansas. At one point Dad slapped her, grabbed her arm and threatened to break it. J.C. barged into the argument and shouted at Dad, "Stop or I'll stop you and call the police!" Dad released Mom and J.C. shouted to him that if he ever hurt Mom again, he would be turned over to the police. I heard this serious argument while in another room and it made me sick to my stomach—a feeling I always had when the arguments turned violent. I also felt like a failure because on the one hand I thought I should do something to stop the violence but I didn't know what to do and was scared to try anyway. Fortunately, J.C. was home and was big enough to make Dad stop. But Dad was humiliated, and he packed a few personal items in a large paper sack and stomped out of the house. He didn't return for several days and we never did learn where he went. In the meantime, J.C. decided to re-enlist in the Army Air Force and moved out permanently. He had been very unhappy with civilian life ever since he returned home and was seriously considering re-enlistment anyway. The confrontation with Dad finalized his decision to do it and he remained in the Air Force as a photographer until he retired many years later.

It wasn't long after Dad returned from his mysterious trip that he put our home up for sale and made other plans for us to move back to Arkansas. He didn't have a job to go to but after seeing the large number of teaching vacancies in the newspaper he subscribed to, he was sure that he could easily find a teaching job. He had selected a location to move to, however. That was Conway, Arkansas a small city with a population of about 6,000 and located almost exactly in the center of the state. Conway was large enough to have good bus and train service yet small enough to provide Dad with the small town atmosphere he yearned for. And Dad and Mom were already familiar with the area surrounding Conway as we had lived close by in Cato from where the Army had moved us. Conway was also close to Jacksonville where he had worked as a guard for the AOP. And, if for some reason there would be the need for services found in a large city, Little Rock was only about 30 miles away. During the time he had left home, he had contacted a couple of real estate agents in Conway and they assured him they could find a furnished apartment to rent with just a few days' notice. The plan was for him to use Conway as a job-hunting command center for a few weeks until he secured a job. He had already sent out letters of inquiry to several small schools close to Conway and had received encouraging responses. Mom was very unhappy with his decisions but had stopped arguing and agreed to move back with him. She liquidated her Sears Roebuck stock and added that money to the other savings she and Dad had accumulated. They figured that their savings would give them plenty of money to live on until Dad got a new job in Arkansas.

Joan and I hoped that no one would buy our house because we didn't want to move back to Arkansas. We had adjusted to the environment in Portland and were very happy and were still thrilled by the newfound luxury of a large house with electricity and running water and no snakes or mosquitoes. We had made good friends in the neighborhood and also at school where I had just finished the fourth grade and Joan had finished the ninth. Our hopes were not realized, however, because our house was sold promptly. Trying to placate us, Dad said we could each have our own suitcase for the train trip. That meant that we would have a total of four suitcases instead of the two suitcases we had when we moved from Arkansas. "You can pack a lot more stuff owning your own suit case," he said. He also promised that when we got settled in Arkansas we could each own a dog but that just made me sad because it reminded me of the dogs we had left behind: Charlie, Penny and Fanny. I wasn't sure I wanted another dog. We never owned one while we lived in Vancouver or Portland and I had gotten used to living without one.

On the last day in our home on Lafayette Street, Dad, Mom, Joan, Bill and I were sitting in our living room joined by Ed Campbell, our next-door neighbor. We didn't own a car while we lived in Portland so Ed offered to drive us to the train station. The new owners agreed that Bill could stay in the house for a few days so he could coordinate with the movers who would put our furniture in storage until we got settled in Arkansas. Then, Bill would move to an apartment in Portland because he had decided not to move with us. We had accumulated a lot of furniture and possessions in the time we had moved from Arkansas and it would take a large moving van to hold it all.

For some puzzling reason, Dad had decided that as a special parting treat we should eat some potato chips so he passed a large bag around but only he and Ed ate them. After a lot of small talk with Ed and lots of devoured potato chips, Dad pulled out his pocket watch and said it was time to go. We said our good byes to Bill and Mom gave him an especially tearful and long goodbye. Then we put our suitcases in Ed's car and drove to the train station.

We drove past the Creston School rubble that was now fenced off and past the gas station where Bill worked. Ed and Dad carried on an animated conversation during the drive to the station, but Mom, Joan and I didn't feel like talking. We arrived at the station on time and we each carried a suitcase and walked briskly along the railroad track where our train was parked. As we passed by the steam engine of our train, I read the name written on its side, "Challenger." This was an important moment that I wanted to remember forever so I deliberately stored the name into my permanent memory. (At the time, I thought the name "Challenger" referred to the specific engine of our train but I learned later that this name designated the engine type, the most powerful steam engine built at that time.)

Looking at Joan sitting in the day car next to me and at my parents sitting across the aisle brought back many memories of our train trip from Arkansas a few years earlier. I think Joan was touched by similar memories because she turned to me and said with an ironic tone; "Sure seems familiar!" and then she chuckled.

The car was full of passengers including a lot of servicemen who were much quieter returning from the war they had just won than the noisy servicemen a few years ago who were going to war. There was also a black family seated a few rows away and they seemed especially deep in thought. They had been told that if they stayed on the train as it passed through the Mason Dixon line, they would have to obey the segregation laws of the south and that included moving to the last car on the train. They were perhaps dreading returning to the disadvantages of segregation but were still drawn by the advantages that they saw in living in the south. Years later I read a black man's description of life while working in the Portland area during World War II. His description hinted at the conflicts caused by living with changing racial social rules: He said, "Our folks never saw so many white folks in one place in their life. White folks never saw so many black folks either. We worked together."

Our train made good progress and before long we were at the Denver train station where we had a four-hour wait while the train was serviced. We ate at the same hot dog stand as we had when we moved from Arkansas. We drank Cokes too but this time none of us believed that drinking it was a sin. Mom still didn't think ladies should sit on stools, however, so she ate her hot dog and drank her Coke standing up next to Dad.

As our train moved south and east from Denver, I spent more time wondering what it was going to be like returning to Arkansas. I still had vivid and unpleasant memories of the weather, the move in the Army trucks and of Lonoke School. Moreover, I had become comfortable with life in Portland including integration and the wet weather. I would miss our large house, my friends and excellent teachers. On the other hand, if we lived on a farm again, there would be lots of land to explore and having a dog to explore it with might be even better. Most important, we would be living in segregation and that should please God according to what I'd been taught. And yet, I was puzzled why so many people in Washington and Oregon, including preachers, disagreed and believed that God didn't want segregation. In any case, I still planned to be a

BORROWED BIBLES

preacher so I could find out for myself what God wanted. But to be a preacher, I needed to learn a lot more so I had been reading the Bible almost every day.

The conductor opened the door and walked slowly down the aisle and announced loudly and officially, "Blacks must move to the last car! Any questions?" I could hear him make the same announcement in the car behind us as he walked through. "Blacks must move to the last car! Any questions?"

CHAPTER **5**

Going to Conway

THE CONWAY REAL estate agent that Dad had been in contact with had a furnished apartment ready for us when we arrived from Portland. He met us at the Conway train station and drove us the short distance to our new home, an apartment on Davis Street. On the way he pointed out a school building and said to Joan and me that school would start the next week and we were lucky because we could easily walk to it. His car was on the small side; the cramped car made the already hot weather seem even hotter and we were all sweating. It was August 1946 and the weather was typical for Arkansas that time of year, about ninety-five degrees with humidity and crawly things to match. If Oregon weather was cold, wet and good for ducks as some people said—Arkansas weather was hot, wet and good for crawly things.

None of us liked the apartment; it was much too small. There was only one bedroom with three beds, a kitchen and a bathroom that was shared with the owner. The owner also agreed to share his telephone with us and that was important since Dad would need a telephone while looking for a job. The bathroom had two entry doors and when the owner used the bathroom, he was supposed to lock our door from the inside for privacy and when he finished, he was supposed to unlock it. Too often, he would forget to unlock it and that led to some very stressful moments. And four people in the bedroom proved as hellish as we had feared. The snoring, breathing, tossing, turning and trips to the bathroom led to little sleep, frayed nerves and cranky dispositions. Although we disliked the apartment, we didn't complain much because we thought our misery would last only a few weeks until Dad got a job.

The kitchen was the social center of our apartment life. We ate there and it also served as a living room and an office for Dad. He would sit at the kitchen table and fill out applications for teaching positions and enclose impressive letters of recommendations. The references were outstanding and that's not surprising because Dad wrote them and signed other people's names. Sometimes he would also include a letter with a doctor's letterhead testifying to his good health. That's not surprising either because he also wrote the medical letters. The references were seldom checked as standard procedure and Dad had learned that school administrators would be desperate to fill positions still vacant close to the beginning of a school year. Since it was August, and most Arkansas schools either started in August or September, his applications for open positions were enthusiastically received. Dad didn't have a college degree but it wasn't required to be a teacher if one had accumulated "appropriate experience" as he had.

Joan and I were surprised when Dad started talking about a teaching job a few months before we left Portland. We knew about his experience as a farmer and a security guard but didn't know he was qualified to be a teacher. We learned, though, that he had taught for over ten years in several small Arkansas schools in the 1920 to 1935 time period. He planned to return to teaching because farming was more of a physical challenge than he wanted, and with the war ended he believed there wouldn't be many jobs for security guards. He hadn't attended college but had received practical business training at the Chillicothe Business College in Chillicothe, Missouri and was one of the few men qualified to teach bookkeeping, shorthand and typing. He had also accumulated enough knowledge of English and History to teach those subjects and his training combined with a handsome, imposing presence made him an appealing candidate. He was also a good fighter and that came in handy because it was a virtual requirement at that time for a new teacher to win a fight with the toughest boy in the school if challenged or lose the support of the community. Dad was challenged and fortunately for his teaching career, he won the fight.

A few days after submitting applications, Dad started to receive phone calls from interested administrators and in a short time he was offered a job that he accepted as principal of a two-room school in the very small town of Republican located about 16 miles from Conway. To get to Republican, one would travel north from Conway on U.S. 65, pass through the small town of Greenbrier 10 miles north of Conway, continue another three miles, turn left on Republican Road, a dirt road, and continue west about another three miles.

The first, second and third grades were taught in one room by Mrs. Josephine Martin and Dad was hired to teach the fourth, fifth and sixth grades in the other room, supervise Mrs. Martin and perform other administrative duties. His compensation was ninety dollars per month and the free use of a teacherage, a house located across the road from the school building. The school year had already started so Dad agreed to go to Republican and take up his duties immediately. He would be a boarder within walking distance of the school. Mom, Joan and I would remain in Conway until our furniture arrived from Portland and then we would join Dad and move into the teacherage. In the meantime, Joan and I would continue to attend Conway public schools where we had recently enrolled.

Normally, it would've been unthinkable to name a town in staunchly Democratic Arkansas "Republican" but the name was selected for political reasons. The original name of the town was Cash Springs named after the Casharago family, Italian emigrants that settled in the area in the 1800s. The residents petitioned for a post office and regular mail service; however, it was found that there was already a town named Cash Springs in Arkansas, so their petition was denied. This perturbed the residents and since William McKinley, a Republican, was president at the time they decided that if they renamed the town and resubmitted the petition it might be granted. They were right; the Republican Post Office was opened on Sept. 20, 1897 but it closed on December 31, 1919. When we moved there in 1946, very few remembered the post office or how the Republican name came about. And when asked how the town got its name, a resident would use self-deprecating humor and say something like, "Cause just like a Republican we're kinda hard to figure out!"

The news spread rapidly that a new school principal and his family would move into the teacherage that had been vacant for several months. This was sensational news for Republican where events out of the ordinary seldom happened and it was even more sensational when people from the outside world moved in. The residents didn't know what to expect and they certainly didn't expect to see the large moving van designed for interstate travel creeping along the narrow, dirt

Republican Road. The van was so tall that it scraped some tree branches and it was so wide that it took up most of the road. Vehicles that met it made sure they pulled over to the roadside as far as possible—and they pulled over fast! The van kept creeping along until it got to within about a mile of the teacherage. Then it stopped at a one-way, wooden bridge and the driver and his helper got out to see if it was strong enough to support the truck. They wisely decided that it wasn't, so they shut off the engine, stood beside the truck and discussed how to solve the problem. The solution was easy and fast. A resident passing by in a pickup truck stopped to find out if anything was wrong. When he learned what the problem was, he offered his pickup to ferry our furniture from the van to the teacherage. It worked perfectly and very shortly the word spread through the town that the new teacher needed help moving in. Shortly, there were several pickup trucks at work ferrying our furniture. The people of Republican went out of their way to be helpful and our family has always been grateful for that. Some people came just to watch the trucks being unloaded and it was an easy way for them to learn what kind of furniture we had. "Looks like we got both helpful neighbors and nosy neighbors," Mom said.

We had arrived at our new home a couple of hours before the pickup trucks did. Dad had lived in Republican by himself for a while so he knew what the house looked like but the rest of us didn't and we were dismayed. It reminded us of the awful features of our farm at Steel Bridge that we had left some four years earlier. There was no indoor plumbing so we would have to use an outhouse again and take a bath in a tub in the back yard again and bring in water from a well again. A wood-burning stove in the living room provided heat, there were cracks in the floor so large that you could look right down to the ground, and the screens on the windows were full of holes. A fundamental fault with the house was its size, consisting of three small bedrooms a living room, a kitchen and no closets. It was immediately clear that the furniture that was being moved from our large Portland house on Lafayette Street would never fit. One bright spot was that there was electricity so we would be able to listen to our radio without worrying about battery life and we would be able to easily read at night. Moreover, there were about 20 acres of woods and interesting briar patches to explore at the back of the house.

GOING TO CONWAY

When Mom digested the full impact of the new home, she bit her lip and softly cried but then she took a deep breath, picked up a broom and began to sweep the floor. Joan and I helped her sweep and I picked up trash that had been left in one of the bedrooms. Dad saw that we were all very unhappy and tried to cheer us up. "You're gonna like this place a lot better after we whitewash it!"

The pickups kept coming and Mom directed the men where to place the furniture as it was unloaded. It didn't take long for the living room, two bedrooms and kitchen to be filled with the furniture we would use day-to-day but there was lots of additional furniture to deal with. Mom decided to use one bedroom for storage only and soon that room was stacked from floor to ceiling. That meant, though, that Joan and I would have to share a bedroom and we were both very unhappy about that turn of events. Needing even more storage space, some furniture was stored on the back porch, some on the front porch and some in an old vacant barn about 50 yards in the back of the house. Dad got rid of some more of the furniture by selling it. He had noticed that several on-lookers liked some of our furniture so he negotiated a good price and sold it on the spot. It was like having an impromptu garage sale.

It took most of the day, but finally all of our furniture had been ferried from the van to our house and the pickup trucks and on-lookers had left. Our move from Portland, Oregon was now complete; we were residents of Republican, Arkansas and our family was alone once again. That evening we ate ice cream and chili, but it didn't help much.

The next Monday I started to school and getting there was easy since it was located right across the road. I walked there with Dad while Joan walked down to the general store to catch a school bus to Greenbrier High School. She was in the tenth grade and I was in the fifth.

I had wondered how Dad was going to teach the fourth, fifth and sixth grades all in the same room. He did it by lining up the grades in separate rows; there were about five students in each row, with the fourth grade on his far right. He would stand directly in front of the fourth grade row, give a lecture to them and assign them work to do while he moved to the fifth grade row and repeated the pattern. Then, he would repeat the pattern to the sixth grade row. And while Dad was teaching his three classes, Mrs. Martin in the room next door was teaching the first, second and third grades using the same process.

I sat in the last seat of the fifth grade row and tried to pay attention to the work assigned to our grade while trying to ignore what Dad said to the other two grades. It was hard to ignore what the other grades were being taught, though, and I was especially interested in the work assigned to the sixth grade because it was more challenging.

After being in the fifth grade for a few days, it was obvious that their class work was very easy. I believed I could do sixth grade work too and to prove it to myself, I started doing it in addition to the fifth grade work; the Oregon schools had prepared me well. I was pleasantly surprised that Dad had come to the same conclusion and after discussing my situation with Mom and gaining her approval, he asked me if I would like to be moved to the sixth grade. I jumped at the chance and this turned out to be one of the most positive events in my life.

Being a teacher's kid was a new experience and a challenge. The other kids looked at me with suspicion and at first they didn't accept me. On the other hand, they weren't mean because they thought Dad might find a way to punish them for it. All the boys had nicknames, and some of the more colorful ones were Stilts, who was much shorter than average; Scales, who had a serious skin problem; and Woody whose knees didn't bend right. I never did figure out why, but I knew things had changed a bit for the better when Woody started calling me "Oregon" and soon the other kids did too. I never did have any real close friends in Republican but Woody became sort of a good friend at least.

Republican was a very dull small town. It consisted of a general store, blacksmith shop and a church. Residents had to go somewhere else to find entertainment and "going to town" was the most entertaining and exciting thing that they could do. It was so exciting that the three words were often pronounced enthusiastically as one word, "goingtotown," much like "damn Yankees" became one word. Sometimes going to town meant going to Greenbrier only about six miles away but it usually meant going to Conway, about sixteen miles away. Kids who were lucky enough to be going to town told the other kids about it in a real snooty way because that just made it a lot more fun. Then, for a few days the kids that weren't going would treat those that were going with great respect and when asked what they were going to do when they got to town, they would usually brag about it. Once, when Mom had just told me that we were going to town, it was my turn to answer, "Well, I'm gonna see a movie, eat ice cream, look at new cars, buy comic books and lots of other things." Everyone knew I was bragging since I didn't have very much money, but they expected me to exaggerate—that was part of the game and we all enjoyed it. After I told the school kids about my trip, Woody gave me a nickel so I could bring him back a Denver Sandwich candy bar. You couldn't buy a Denver Sandwich in Republican's general store but you could buy one in at least three stores in Conway.

Going to town in 1940's was a big problem for some of the residents. Not every one had a car and there were no public buses that traveled the dirt roads leading to our homes. Quite a few folks still used wagons pulled either by horses or mules and a few men rode on tractors. There was a wide variety of tractors including several models of the red Farmall, a few green John Deere tractors with engines that made a distinctive "pung-pung-pung" sound and gray Ford or Ferguson tractors that couldn't be told apart until you got up close. It was an interesting sight on Saturday to see a mixture of cars, wagons, tractors, horses, and mules all going to town. For those of us that didn't have any vehicles or animals there was still another way to go. We could ride in Howie's "chicken coop."

It wasn't really a chicken coop but it did look like one and my parents called it that. It was a black wooden box bolted to the bed of a pickup truck. There were no windows in the box and the door at the back had a latch that could only be turned from outside. The latch was usually locked and only Howie and members of his family had a key. Inside the box were two benches that ran lengthwise with the truck bed and faced each other. The idea was to get six people in the box, three on a bench, and then Howie would close and lock the door, pocket the key, and drive the truck to town. For this service, he would charge a quarter per passenger for a round trip from Republican to Conway. Howie would make this trip on certain Saturdays, if he felt like it, and if he had a full load. I'm not sure how the grown-ups let Howie know which Saturday they wanted to go to Conway, but the would-be passengers would meet at the local blacksmith shop at about 9:00 a.m. and, more often than not, Howie would drive down from his farm and load them up. During the week, the truck hauled all sorts of farm material from fence posts to cow manure, which was used as an all-around fertilizer. And sometimes the truck would be used to haul chickens and that seemed real appropriate. On Sundays, Howie's father would haul people to church at no charge. It was a good, general-purpose truck.

We had been warned about Howie. When we first moved to Republican, a group of three local women called on Mom to welcome us to the neighborhood and to bring her up to date on the community gossip. After the small talk ended, the women told Mom that there were two people that we had to careful of: Mrs. White and Howie. Mrs. White lived only about a mile up the road from us and was sort of a witch. All three women had seen her turn rabbits into cats and they said her house was full of cats that used to be rabbits. They also suspected that Mrs. White could turn children into cats and although they never saw her do it they warned Mom to keep Joan and me far away from her just to be on the safe side. As far as Howie was concerned, I heard them tell her that he would sometimes strip down to his underwear, grab his pistol, drive his truck around the countryside and fire his pistol in the air for hours at a time. No one knew why he did this. I thought this was strange but I didn't think I would ever have anything to do with Howie in any case, so I didn't worry about it. That was before I learned that Howie drove the chicken coop.

Howie was about thirty years old and the only bachelor in the community who still lived with his mother and father. Besides driving the truck to town on Saturdays, when he felt like it, he worked on his parents' farm a few hours a week but did nothing else to make a living. His farm was not too far from where I lived and I would sometimes walk by and find him sitting on the porch just staring in space. Once, I passed by at dinnertime and he was standing on the porch eating salmon right out of the can with a spoon so big that it would barely fit in the can. On this occasion he seemed more alert than usual so I greeted him but he didn't answer; however, he did stop eating and stared at me until I was out of sight. Another time I met him while I was walking on one of the dirt roads and he was driving the truck toward me. I waved to him, but he ignored me.

He had dropped out of school in the fourth grade and could barely read or write. He was content to stay home and do a few chores around the house or work in the fields with his father. When he became eighteen, he left Arkansas and went to Indiana for what was first thought to be for good, but he returned after a few months and never left home again. His father taught him to drive the truck when Howie was about twenty and the two of them built the wooden "chicken coop" and bolted it on the truck bed. There was a time when Howie would occasionally take a girl for a drive but no girl ever went out with him more than once and after his incident with Agnes, girls didn't go with him at all.

Agnes was a very quiet, plain looking, girl in the tenth grade who had never dated until Howie asked her to go with him to the general store. One Saturday evening each month the store would stay open until eight and it was common on that night for boys to take girls there, buy them a soda and candy, sit and talk until the store closed and then drive the girls back home by nine. On the Saturday evening Howie drove Agnes to the store he was as quiet as usual and since Agnes almost never spoke, the entire trip was made in silence. As they got close to the store, though, Howie said, "No, we're gonna do somethin else tonight." He made a U turn and raced to a small lane about a mile away. Shortly after he turned down the lane, he cut the engine and reached out for Agnes. She was terrified, opened her door and tried to run away. Howie's hand caught the back of her collar and ripped her blouse down the back. She jumped from the truck, and ran down the lane screaming with her torn blouse flapping. Howie didn't know what to do, so he watched her run until she was out of sight. Then he drove home, ate a can of salmon and went to bed.

It was reported in the community gossip, that the next morning Howie was eating breakfast with his parents when Agnes' father, Roy, pushed open the front door and barged in holding a rifle. Yelling, "I'm gonna kill you." He ran into the kitchen and placed the barrel of the rifle against Howie's head. Howie's parents pleaded for him not to kill Howie but Roy yelled at the top of his voice, "No, this son-of-a-bitch needs to die," and he pulled the trigger. There was a loud click as the hammer hit the empty rifle chamber. Howie's mother fainted when she heard the click but Roy continued to shout, "If you ever go near Agnes again, I'll put a bullet in this rifle, hunt you down and kill you like a dog—understand?" Howie was too scared to speak but he nodded that he understood and Howie's father said weakly, "He won't." With that, Roy stormed out of the house.

Howie did have one good friend, Ed, who lived close by and was a good ten years younger. Howie didn't talk or laugh much or show much emotion of any kind unless he was with Ed. Then, the two of them would talk almost nonstop and sometimes Howie would laugh so hard he would bend over and then Ed would start giggling and snorting. I never did hear what they said to each other because if I, or any other kid, came near them, they would stop talking until we were out of earshot.

It was Saturday morning and I had looked forward to the day so much that I had hardly slept. I was going to Conway with Mom. It was like the night before Christmas and Christmas morning. I woke up earlier than usual and dressed rapidly but being very careful to put Woody's nickel and my own nickel in a pocket without a hole in it. I walked into the kitchen, stuffed some bacon into a biscuit and wolfed it down while standing up. Mom was clearing the breakfast table even though Dad was still sitting there drinking coffee. He was not going to town with us but was staying home with Joan who was still in bed recovering from the flu. Dad couldn't make up his mind whether to be mad about staying home or not. On the one hand he was irritated that Mom could so easily go without him but on the other hand he looked forward to a day of peace and quiet with just Joan in the house. "So you're going with her are you?" he asked me. Even though he knew the answer I said, "Yes," because that was how we talked about things. Mom said, "Go out and wait, I'll be there in a minute."

I waited by the mailbox, which was about fifty feet from our house, and right next to the dirt road so the mail carrier could just lean out his car window and put our mail in the box. Although it was still early in the morning, it felt like it would be a very hot day. At least as hot as the last few days that were over ninety and the kids at school said it had been so hot that some of the ponds were beginning to dry up. I began to think about eating ice cream in Conway and that made me happier since the hot weather would make it taste better. I also looked forward to just *being* in Conway again. Now it seemed like a large, exciting city while a few months ago when we arrived from Portland it seemed so small and dull.

As Mom left the house and walked toward me, Dad shouted after her, "I'll want supper by six! You hear that?" Mom shook her head slowly side-to-side and said "shh-uh" which she always did when she wanted to express disgust. I figured that we would leave Conway about three thirty or four and arrive back in Republican by four thirty at the latest so it would be easy to have supper made by six.

It was only about a quarter of a mile from our house to the blacksmith shop where Howie was to pick us up and it was early so there was no need to walk fast. We settled into an easy stroll. I didn't want Mom to know that I was beginning to be a little afraid of the ride with Howie, but I couldn't help asking, "Why couldn't we hitch a ride in a neighbor's car?" She answered, "I won't ask anyone and I won't beg anyone for a ride. This way we don't have to ask anyone and that's that." And it was too.

We soon walked past the schoolhouse that always looked out of place on the weekend when no one was there and it seemed like only a few minutes ago, and not a few days ago, when Woody gave me a nickel so I could buy him a Denver Sandwich. I reached in my pocket and was reassured that his nickel as well as mine was still there.

Another fifty feet and on our right we passed by the public well where anyone could get water. Every school morning would begin with two kids going to the well to bring back two buckets of water for the day. On real hot days another trip would be taken in the afternoon. It was considered a privilege to be one of the kids that carried the water.

The three buildings of the Republican business section were another hundred feet from the public well and at the rate we were walking we'd be at the blacksmith shop in plenty of time. To the left of the blacksmith shop, was the general store and as usual there were wagons parked outside and men sitting on the store bench talking and dipping snuff. The third public building was the church, on the right of the blacksmith shop. About six months earlier, the congregation had selected a new preacher, Reverend Knox, that they hoped would bring new life to the church. He said he had never seen as many sinners as there were in Republican, but he promised to root them out and make

BORROWED BIBLES

them all come back to Jesus before Christmas. Dad had heard good things about Reverend Knox even before we moved to Republican and had hopes that he would be the kind of preacher that preached right—even though he was not a Church of Christ preacher. Our family visited the church the first Sunday after our move and Dad was impressed, "He knows the Bible and knows how to preach it. And I like the way he puts the fear of God in people. I just wish they didn't use that heathen piano though." So Dad gave Joan and me permission to attend the church on an on-going basis but he urged us to just listen to the sermons and ignore the piano playing. He said that he and Mom wouldn't be going every Sunday but only from time to time but that I should go every Sunday since I planned on being a preacher someday. Dad added that he wouldn't be conducting church services on the front porch as long as Reverend Knox preached like a true Christian.

The dirt road we were walking on continued between the blacksmith shop and the general store and connected to U.S. 65, a paved highway about three miles away. Making a right turn on U.S. 65 and traveling south would lead first to Greenbrier and then Conway. This was the route that we would soon be taking in the chicken coop.

There were four other people including a baby that were waiting when Mom and I arrived. I had never before seen the pudgy woman who was holding the baby and she bounced it by shifting her weight first to one leg and then to the other. The bouncing did the trick because the baby was sound asleep and I took that to be a good sign. The other two passengers were a high school girl named Anna Sumner and her father. I had seen them at church several times and had noticed that they kept to themselves and seldom talked to anyone except the preacher. Mom whispered in my ear that Anna was wearing a dress made out of flour sacks. I recognized the Magic Millers pattern that Joan and I used to wear and was real glad that we now had enough money to buy regular clothes. Mr. Sumner was holding a coffee can and he would regularly spit a stream of tobacco juice into it.

The pudgy woman said, "Her name's Peggy," referring to the baby who was still asleep. No one responded to her comment and no one said anything else. We just stood around and waited until we saw Howie's truck coming towards us. "Give this to him yourself," Mom said, handing me a quarter for my fare.

There was someone in the passenger's seat of Howie's truck and when it got close enough I could see that it was Ed. The truck came to a stop about six feet from where we were standing and both Howie and Ed jumped out and walked to the rear of the truck. They left the cab doors open and I could see a pistol on the truck floor. I knew that Mom saw it too because her eyes widened and she bit her bottom lip. I figured that she would cancel our trip because of Howie's reputation for stripping to his underwear and shooting the revolver in the air, but instead she walked to the back of the truck where Howie had unlocked and opened the door to the coop. I knew Mom would try to be the last one to board because she didn't think it was ladylike to climb into a truck and the fewer people that saw her from behind while she was climbing the better. Since I was standing next to her, I figured I would be the next-to-last to board but Howie held out one hand for the quarter fare and with the other hand he pointed to me, "You first," he said. Ed giggled and snorted.

I boosted myself to the door of the coop and bent over so I could crawl to my part of the bench. Even with the back door open, it was pretty dark inside but I could see a small woman on the right hand bench at the end next to the cab. It was Mrs. Whitly, a widow, whom Howie had picked up on his way to town. I made my way forward and sat next to her. She glanced at me but otherwise ignored me and I didn't say anything to her either. I noticed a terrible smell as soon as I entered the coop and I could make out the odor of chicken manure, dust and strong perfume worn by Mrs. Whitly. It was pretty hard to breathe just right because if I took a normal sized breath the smell made me gag but a small breath didn't give me enough air and that would make me gag too. Mr. Sumner came in next and took a seat on the bench right in front of Mrs. Whitly. As soon as he was settled, he spat a stream of tobacco juice in his coffee can and soon the smell of tobacco was added to the other smells. Then Anna boarded, and sat next to her father. She faced me and since the coop was so small our knees almost touched. The pudgy woman came in next and as soon as she was settled, Howie, who had held the baby while she was climbing aboard, handed it back to her. Peggy was still asleep but I wondered if she would be able to keep on sleeping with all the bad smells. As I had guessed, Mom was the last to board and she sat next to me. We all had to sit with our upper bodies at an angle if we didn't want our shoulders to touch, but there was no place to put our feet or knees so they didn't touch. Now that the coop was fully loaded it was really getting hard to breathe.

Howie slammed the door shut and locked it, which blocked out all the direct light, but some sunlight streamed in through cracks at the door and through a few small knotholes. The inside of the coop was about as dark as a clear, starlit night.

I could hear Howie and Ed walking back towards the cab, getting in and closing their doors. Howie started the engine and yelled out the window to the men looking at us from the general store, "We're goingtotown!" and Ed thumped on the side of his door and echoed, "Goingtotown!" The pudgy woman said, "Peggy, you're goingtotown, whatcha think of that?" No one else said anything.

With the truck moving, the air inside got even worse because exhaust gas and road dust was seeping in. I was feeling more and more like I was going to throw up and wished that I hadn't eaten the bacon for breakfast or at least that I had sat down to eat. Mr. Sumner spat some more tobacco.

The dirt road hadn't been graded for over a year so there were lots of ruts and ridges in it and we felt each one of them since the benches had no padding. I was being thrown around and couldn't help slamming against Mom and Mrs. Whitly—once I lurched forward and hit Anna. On one of the big bumps I noticed that the coop banged against the truck bed and that meant the anchor bolts had come loose. I wondered how dangerous that was and whether or not Howie knew they were loose.

Between gagging on the odors and being thrown around, I could feel my stomach moving towards my throat and I was getting real dizzy. I prayed to God to please let me hold my food in. If I could just hold my food in for a little while, I thought, we would get to U.S. 65 and then we should have a smooth ride at least. "Oops, guess what little Peggy just did!" the pudgy woman said. No one responded to her comment and no one said anything because everyone had figured out what Peggy just did.

I twisted my upper body and looked out a knothole that was above my shoulder and saw that we were passing by the Duggar farm. That meant that we were close to the stop sign at the intersection of our dirt road and U.S. 65. Then, we would stop for a little while which might help clear out some of the dust and exhaust fumes. But suddenly, the truck accelerated rapidly and made a right turn so sharp that the people on the left side of the coop were thrown on our laps. Howie hadn't stopped, but had floored the accelerator and drove right through the stop sign. Peggy was still asleep, though, and that was a good sign.

As I had hoped, the ride was a lot smoother on the concrete highway and the road dust was much less but the exhaust fumes got worse. And the sun was heating up the coop.

I looked out the knothole again and was surprised to see how fast we were going—I had no idea that Howie's truck could go so fast. We lurched to the left and accelerated to even a higher speed and I could see that we were passing another truck. We were going faster and faster and then we swerved rapidly to the right to get back in our lane. My head was spinning; I was gagging and closed my eyes. We swerved again to the left and immediately back to the right. For some reason that I couldn't figure out, Howie's driving became wilder and I heard a muffled, "Gonna die!" from the cab along with some giggles and snorts. Another swerve to the left and then a rapid and big swerve to the right sent all the people on the left side of the coop over to our side. Then I felt the coop starting to lean and I could tell it was beginning to fall off the truck bed. So could everybody else because there were screams and shouts for help. The coop hit the highway with such force that I thought everyone would be killed but the surprising thing was that the coop didn't break open. It just skidded along the highway on its side until we hit the grassy hill that was alongside the road. We were tumbling, tumbling and everyone inside was bouncing off the walls and the floor—arms and legs seemed to be everywhere. Anna was screaming. The tobacco can was flying. The coop was tumbling, tumbling. In the distance there was laughter, giggles and snorts and then I heard gunshots. My head was spinning, and Peggy was crying. Then, we stopped skidding and tumbling and came to a rest with the coop on its side. No one but me moved and I didn't know if everyone else was dead or unconscious. I crawled over Mom and the pudgy woman and was relieved to discover they were still breathing. I kept crawling until I got to the door. I pounded at it with my hands and kicked it with my feet, but I couldn't open it. I believed we would all die locked up in a black box on an Arkansas hillside with the sun beating down on us.

The door opened and the bright sun streamed inside. Howie and Ed stood at the door opening and behind them Saturday morning traffic was moving on the streets of Conway. The coop hadn't come off after all, no one was hurt and Peggy was still sound asleep. Instead of being in an accident, I had become delirious and passed out and it had been so dark inside the coop nobody noticed, not even Mom.

We climbed down from the coop as fast as possible and everyone stretched and took deep breaths but no one besides me seemed to be sick. I was the last one off and was still very dizzy and sick to my stomach. Outside the coop I stood bent over and held my stomach to help keep my food down. Howie pointed at me and laughed while Ed snorted. Then, Howie announced to us, "We're going back at four and I ain't gonna come looking for you."

Mom could see that I was very sick, (she told me later that my skin had turned dark yellow), so she helped me to a bench in front of a cattle-feed store a few feet away from where Howie had parked his truck. "You sit here, I have to run some errands and then I'll be back for you."

The bright sunlight felt wonderful and I couldn't get enough of the fresh air. I took one deep breath after another and sat on the bench with my eyes closed, breathing fresh air and trying to get the knots in my stomach untied. I hoped there were no other kids from Republican in town to see me just sitting on the bench looking sick.

"Are you OK, Lester, and why are you sitting here and why are those cigarette butts down at your feet?" It was the voice of Reverend Knox our preacher from Republican who usually came to Conway every Saturday.

"I'm OK, sir."

"Well, you don't look good. Looks to me like you've been smoking and now you're sick. If you've started to smoke you've started down the road to hell and God has punished you and you'll never be a preacher! Do you see that?"

"I'm OK, sir."

He ignored what I said and kept on talking.

"And you haven't been baptized either have you? You come to church a lot and that's good and you want to be a preacher and that's good but it won't do you any good if you die before you're baptized cause you'll end up in hell anyway."

I looked up and could see that his eyes were accusing me even louder than his voice. I was so sick, though, that I didn't care very much what he thought or said even if he was the preacher.

"No, sir. I haven't been baptized."

"Tomorrow–in church tomorrow–I want you to stand up and then walk up that aisle, ask for God's forgiveness in Jesus' name and be baptized. Otherwise, if you die, you'll go straight to hell and stay there forever so you better stop smoking and get baptized. Now, Jesus truly does love you and I want you to get prepared to meet him. You understand?"

He didn't wait for an answer but turned and walked away. Now, on top of being sick I was afraid I might die and go to hell. It didn't seem right to be sent to hell, especially forever, for smoking when I hadn't smoked; however, the preacher was a man of God and I had been taught that preachers always spoke the truth. On the other hand, he didn't know what the truth was this time. I didn't want to take any chances, though, so right then I made up my mind to get baptized on Sunday and I hoped I wouldn't die before.

About fifteen minutes after the preacher walked away, I left the bench and went to a nearby grocery store and bought a Denver Sandwich for Woody like I had promised him. My legs were wobbly and my head was still spinning so I hurried back to the bench and sat down again.

After waiting about another hour, a car pulled up close to where I was sitting and I could see Mom in the back seat. She rolled down the window and said, "Get in, we're goin home." She had bumped into a neighbor and his wife who had driven to Conway in their car. She had swallowed her pride and asked for a ride back to Republican rather than go back with Howie.

We arrived home about two and Dad seemed happy because he probably thought we came home so early because Mom was worried that his supper wouldn't be on time. And even though supper was on time I was still too sick to eat anything and went to bed early.

On Sunday morning I was still sick so I was allowed to sleep late and miss church. I got up about ten and although I hadn't eaten for over a day, I wasn't hungry. It was a good thing that Mom and Dad didn't know about my run-in with the preacher or they would have made me get up at the regular time and go to church, sick or not. All day long, I suffered from the strong smells of the chicken coop and waves of nausea passed through me. Finally, by Sunday evening, I started to feel better. I ate a few crackers for supper and then went to bed.

Monday morning as I walked across the road to school, I saw Woody and some of the other kids waiting on the school ground to meet me. I gave Woody his Denver Sandwich and answered their questions about what I did in Conway, "Well, I ate a lot of ice cream, and a Denver Sandwich just like Woody's, and then I walked all over Conway, and looked at new cars, and lots of other things."

[Courtesy Faulkner County Arkansas Museum]

The Republican, Arkansas School House

This was a two-room schoolhouse. The door and window on the left was for the classroom used by the first, second and third grades. The room on the right had its own door and window and was used by the fourth, fifth and sixth grades taught by my Dad during the 1946-47 school year. Dad was also the principal of the school and reported to the superintendent of the Greenbrier, Arkansas school system located about six miles away.

CHAPTER 6

Questions

IT HAD BEEN a few weeks since my trip to Conway in the chicken coop and school with Dad as my sixth grade teacher had settled into a routine. But my Sundays were different. Reverend Knox had noticed that I wasn't in church the Sunday after my trip and even though I told him I had been too sick to attend, I could tell that he didn't believe me and he became very hostile. He had made a pledge to have all the sinners in Republican baptized by Christmas and he had missed that goal. He included me in the group of sinners that refused to get baptized and that added to his hostility toward me. I reacted to his behavior by avoiding him. I still went to church but I always sat as close to the door as I could and would leave without talking to him like I had in the past. I hadn't told my parents about him falsely accusing me of smoking in Conway or about him pressuring me to get baptized or that our relationship had taken a bad turn.

School was over for the day and I was walking across the road to our house with Dad when I noticed Reverend Knox standing by his car parked in front of our house. He said, "Mr. Good, could I have a word with you?"

"You bet," Dad said, "Come on in the house with us and visit a bit."

"Well, I'd like it if I could talk to you out here if that's all right and just you and me if that's all right."

Dad told me, "Go on in the house, Junior, I'll be along in a minute."

I went inside and hurried to the front window so I could watch what would happen between the Reverend and Dad. Mom was watching too and had been ever since the Reverend parked his car in front of our house. She hadn't walked out to talk to him because she didn't think

BORROWED BIBLES

that would be ladylike so she waited for him to come up to the house but he never did. Joan ignored the event because she was completely absorbed in making a new dress that she badly needed. The Reverend was too far away for me to hear what he was telling Dad but it was pretty clear there was serious talking going on. At one point he shook his finger in Dad's face and I knew Dad wouldn't like that. They continued to talk for quite a while but then they shook hands, and the Reverend drove away. Dad came into the house and said, "Tish, Joan, Junior, come on and sit down I wanna talk to you. I mainly wanna talk to you, Junior, but I want everybody to listen—Joan, stop your sewing and sit over here."

Dad looked straight at me and said:

"Reverend Knox had some pretty serious things to say and I gotta figure out what to do about it. The first thing he said is that when he was in Conway recently, he saw you sittin on a bench looking real sick and there were cigarette butts by your feet. He said you were smokin, which is a sin when someone your age does it, and the smokin made you sick. Now, how about it?"

"I wasn't smokin! I've never smoked. It was the stink inside the chicken coop that made me sick—I was sick to my stomach!"

Mom spoke up, "He didn't smoke. I was with him 'till I left him on the bench cause he was so sick. It was that coop that made him sick—I could see that plainly cause his skin was pasty and yellow. He didn't have money for cigarettes and there wasn't any smell on his breath. That bench already had cigarette butts around it when he sat down and I saw them. The Reverend is just plain wrong!"

Joan had waited until Mom and Dad couldn't see her do it and then gave me one of her special, sneaky grins. It was her way of communicating to me that she just might speak up and say that she had seen me smoking just to get me in trouble. And that would get me in big trouble too because Dad would believe whatever she said even if it differed from what Mom said and even if it wasn't the truth. She was only teasing me though and fortunately didn't say anything.

Dad said, "OK, then, I guess Junior didn't do it and that ends that. Now let's get to somethin else. The Reverend has noticed that you kids haven't been baptized and he's asked you both to get it done but you've ignored and avoided him. Now, I didn't know anything about this but let me be clear; I don't want you to be baptized in his church. You both are gonna be baptized in the Church of Christ. Now, there isn't one here but we aren't gonna stay here much longer. We're gonna be movin, and sooner or later we'll live close to a Church of Christ. I told the Reverend all that and he didn't like it but that's the way it's gotta be."

I wasn't surprised that we would be moving because we moved about once a year ever since I could remember and Mom said they had been doing it since they were married. The Republican school year was coming to an end in about six weeks so I figured we would move a little bit after that but I didn't know where to.

Dad continued, "Now another thing about baptizing is that it doesn't count unless you're old enough to understand and believe the Bible. Faith has to come first then we can get to the baptizing. In the Church of Christ you gotta be at least 12 years old so Junior you have about two more years to go. But Joan, if we had the right church around here, you could be baptized now. Reverend Knox said he baptizes kids as young as four and he said that's common in the Baptist church but I don't think he's right. I don't recall any other Baptist church baptizing that young."

Mom said, "Well, I was baptized in the Baptist church and I had to wait till I was 12. I never heard of the Baptist church baptizing as young as four either except for the soft shell Baptists who will do most anything. The Reverend may be hard shell in some things but he's soft shell when it comes to baptizing. That's mighty strange!"

Dad leaned toward Joan and me for emphasis. "You two aren't goin to Reverend Knox's church anymore. It isn't right that he pressured you into gettin baptized without checking with your Mom or me first. And it sure isn't right for him to be baptizing children younger than 12. But I want you to spend the time on Sunday that you would've spent in church reading the Bible here at home instead. Junior, I know you're reading it during the week anyway but I want you to add the Sunday time. And you've been readin in a scattered fashion, but now I want you to start at the beginning, at Genesis, and keep on readin till you finish the whole Bible. And I want you to keep a notebook and write down any questions you come up with. You can get your questions answered as soon as we move and find a Church of Christ preacher. Readin the Bible all the way through and gettin your questions answered is gonna help you a lot when you go to preacher's college. I can help but I won't have as much time as I used to cause I'm going to work on finishing college and that means doing a lot of homework at night and the weekend. Joan, you're further along in readin than Junior so you can read what you want and you don't have to keep a notebook cause I know you don't want to be a preacher. It's hard for a woman to get to be a preacher anyway. Now, religion is mighty important but so is eatin and I'm hungry. Tish, it's time you and Joan went to the kitchen and got supper ready."

I was pleased I didn't have to go to church anymore and that I'd have time on Sunday to read the Bible without being disturbed. I had been reading it off and on but now I would get really organized and make it a regular habit. And starting at the beginning and reading it all the way through should help me understand it. I had jumped around in my reading a lot—sometimes I would read the Old Testament and sometimes the New and I found some interesting things but it raised a lot of questions. I was especially interested in all the war stories I found in the Old Testament. They reminded me of the hand-to-hand battles we had just fought in World War II with the Japanese on the Pacific Islands. And my favorite Bible battle, the battle of Jericho, reminded me of the fascinating battles our cavalry had when the Indians attacked our forts. It must have been scary being one of the soldiers inside the walls of Jericho watching the build up of the Israeli forces under the leadership of Joshua, particularly since God was personally telling Joshua what to do. And the instructions were very detailed. First, the Israeli soldiers, about 40,000 of them, were to be circumcised with a sharp knife. Now I had only recently learned what circumcision was from a classmate who talked about it at school, and it seemed to me that it would be very painful and I wondered how this would affect their fighting ability. Anyway, sometime after the circumcisions, the soldiers were ordered to march around the city once a day for six days, which no doubt increased the pressure on the soldiers and residents inside the walls. But the real action came on the seventh day when the Israelis marched around the city seven times. Then, seven of their priests, followed by the Ark of the Covenant, blew a long blast on seven trumpets made of ram horns and the 40,000 soldiers, upon a command from Joshua, gave a loud shout. That did it; the walls that had protected Jericho came tumbling down and lay flat. The Israeli soldiers charged in and used their swords to kill every living thing including women and children, with the exception of one woman and her family who had recently helped Israeli spies. They also killed all the livestock and took all the gold, silver and iron objects as an offering to God. When the killing and looting was over, they set fire to what was left of Jericho. I thought this story was very interesting, but it raised some questions that I hoped to get answered some day. It puzzled me that earlier God had given Moses a set of Ten Commandments including one not to kill; however, at Jericho He was not only directing Joshua to kill but also giving him details on how to kill. When was it all right with God for us to kill? Why were the women and children killed? Why was the livestock killed? I believed I had these questions only because I hadn't read the Bible in the right way. The story of the Jericho battle might be clearer after reading the first five books of the Old Testament that preceded it.

The next Sunday I hurried through breakfast so I could start my Bible study as Dad had ordered. I was hoping to sit in the living room corner with the good sunlight but Joan already had that corner occupied and was holding her Bible. She gave me a triumphant smile as I walked by her. I took the corner opposite her, sat down and turned to Genesis. She told me, "I'm sure glad I don't have to read it all the way through again. I did it once and it took me forever and I mostly didn't understand it. Even if I could be, I'd never be a preacher." She then started turning the pages somewhere around the middle of the Bible but I could tell she was just killing time to satisfy Mom and Dad—she really wasn't interested in learning about the word of God. Unlike me, she wanted to go to Reverend Knox's church but not because she wanted to hear him preach. It was because there was a boy named Max that attended the church and she had taken a keen liking to him and it seemed he felt the same. Max, like Joan, was in the tenth grade in the Greenbrier High School and rode the bus every school day from Republican with Joan so there were lots of opportunities for the two to talk and flirt. Lately, Joan had tried to get up enough courage to ask Mom and Dad if Max could come to the house some evening and take her for a walk but so far she had held her tongue. On this day, however,

Joan didn't have to worry about Mom and Dad watching her closely because they had also finished breakfast and were in the backyard talking quietly so Joan and I couldn't hear them. I believed they were talking details about our next move.

I knew that the first part of Genesis was about God creating everything that there is but I planned to hurry through that part and get to the story about Noah and the ark. My Sunday school teacher had talked about Noah and showed us a picture of the animals walking up a ramp into the ark and I thought that was almost as interesting as the Bible war stories. I opened my Bible and started reading and I was right; page one of Genesis was about God creating light, the earth, day and night, the dry land, the water, the sun, stars and all the living things. Then, He created Adam and Eve who fell into sin when they ate fruit from a certain tree. The descendants of Adam and Eve were named next by the use of a lot of "begats" and that didn't interest me very much until I got to Lamech who begat a son that he named Noah. Sometime after Noah was five hundred years old, God saw how wicked the people of the earth had become and this grieved Him so much that He vowed to destroy every living thing except Noah, his wife, his three sons and their wives. God spared Noah because he was a just man, he walked with God and he was perfect in his generation. God said that he would carry out His destruction by creating a great flood; therefore, in order to survive, Noah was instructed to build an ark three hundred cubits long, fifty cubits wide and thirty cubits high. I had wanted to know how large the ark really was ever since my Sunday school teacher showed us a picture of it but the description in Genesis didn't help because I didn't know how long a cubit was. I thought Joan might be able to help me so I asked her about the length of a cubit.

"I don't remember exactly but it had something to do with how long a forearm is but I forgot whose forearm they were talking about so it could be most anything as far as I know. I guess you're reading about Noah's ark but how come you wanta know how long a cubit is anyway?"

"So I can figure out how big the ark was. I just wanta know—was it as big as those cargo ships we saw when we lived up in Portland? Or was it more like the size of those houseboats we've seen here in Arkansas on the rivers?"

QUESTIONS

"Well, I just don't know, you'll have to ask Mom or Dad but I expect it was pretty big in order to hold all those animals. Now don't bother me anymore cause I'm reading the Bible too." What she was really doing, though, was just pretending to read while she thought about going for a walk with Max.

I wrote down the question about the cubit in my notebook and then continued to read about God's instructions to Noah. In Genesis 6:19 He told Noah that regarding living things, he was to bring two of every sort into the ark, male and female, in order to keep them alive during the flood. This seemed clear and sensible to me but then very shortly I got to Genesis 7:2 and there Noah was told to take by sevens every clean beast, male and female, and take two of every beast not clean, male and female. I was very puzzled by this and wondered if I had made a mistake so I reread the two verses in Genesis and sure enough, it seemed that God told Noah to take a different number of animals in just a short period of time. I thought about asking Joan about this but she had made it plain that she didn't want to be bothered anymore and besides she probably couldn't explain the different numbers anyway. Up to this point I had read pretty fast so I could get to the story about Noah and I wondered if I had missed something. I decided to back up, start all over at page one and read Genesis again.

On my second reading of Genesis, I read it much slower and noticed things I had completely missed before that raised several questions. In Genesis 1:3 God said on the first day of creation, "Let there be light." But it was on the fourth day of creation, that God made the sun and the stars as written in Genesis 1:16. How could there have been light before the sun and stars were made? And at one place it was written that man was created before the vegetation and trees but in another place it was written that man was created after the vegetation and trees.

I was embarrassed and discouraged. I had been reading the Bible and thinking about what I had read for over an hour. I had read parts of Genesis twice but still had only finished the first seven chapters that ended on page eight. I knew that Genesis had a total of fifty chapters and with the rate I was reading and thinking it would take me forever to finish Genesis—let alone the whole Bible, just as Joan had said. I stopped reading and closed my Bible in frustration. I needed to get my questions answered because until I did, it didn't make any sense to keep on reading and coming up with even more questions. I didn't want to wait until we found a Church of Christ preacher to help either. Instead, I planned to ask either Mom or Dad my questions the first chance I got. I thought Mom would be the best to ask since she had been raised to believe all the Old Testament whereas Dad and the Church of Christ believed only part of it. After she and Dad came in from the back yard, I waited until she was alone and then asked her the questions I had about Genesis.

She explained that God could do anything and wasn't limited like man is. So, if God wanted to make light before there was a sun or stars, then it was easy for Him to do it just like Genesis said He did. Concerning the number of animals that Noah brought into the ark, Mom said both numbers were right. That is, the seven clean animals were divided into three pairs, male and female, for a total of six clean animals plus one additional clean animal that Noah used as a burnt offering because God found their aroma pleasing. God didn't like the animals that weren't clean nearly as much as the clean animals and that's why Noah didn't have to save as many or make burnt offerings with them. Mom said that even with the explanations in the Bible, however, it could be hard to figure out God sometimes because He wasn't a human. But if the Bible said it, then it was true whether we could figure it out or not.

What she said helped my understanding a lot, but it also caused me to wonder why God created animals that weren't clean in the first place. I could see, though, that Mom was getting tired of talking about God so while I had the chance I asked one more question:

"What's a cubit?"

"Well, I remember that there was more than one answer for that but if you're askin about those numbers for Noah's ark, then most people say a cubit is eighteen inches."

I was pretty good with arithmetic so I used the information that Mom gave me about the cubit to figure out that Noah's ark was 450 feet long, 75 feet wide and 45 feet high. For the first time I had some idea about the size of the ark was but I knew even a better way to get a feeling about how big it was.

The property we were renting in Republican used to be a small farm. There was still a barn behind our house and some of our furniture was stored there. Beyond the barn there was a large empty pasture that had a few trees in one of the corners. I got the idea to mark out an area on the pasture that would be about the same size as the bottom of the ark. I used one of the trees as one corner and then stepped out a distance of 450 feet, using a three-foot long step I had been taught to make, and placed several rocks to mark another corner. I gathered up rocks and branches and used them to mark two other corners to complete an area about 450 feet long and 75 feet wide, the same as the bottom of Noah's ark. Then I climbed up on the roof of the barn to get a better look at what I'd marked and was amazed. The ark was much bigger than I had imagined and I was sure it could hold a lot of animals especially since Noah had been told to build three different levels inside it. I looked at it for a long time and imagined animals living in all the rooms while Noah and his family moved around the ark taking care of them.

I hadn't noticed that Dad had come to the barn but as I started to climb down from the roof he asked, "What're you doing up there? Get down here!"

"Dad, see those markers I put down in the pasture? That's about the size of the bottom of Noah's ark. I got the idea for using corner markers from watching our neighbor use them for a barn he was planning. I just wanted to see how big it really was and I thought I could get a better look by standing on the roof."

Dad chuckled and said, "Well, I'll be! That's a good way of lookin at it and I hadn't really thought about how long 450 feet actually is. And it's long! Remember, I was a shipyard guard when we lived in Washington and the cargo ships being built were about 440 feet long. Well, Noah's ark was even a bit longer than that."

"You said some parts of the Old Testament are true and some aren't. Is the part about Noah's ark true?"

"Yes, but I don't think Noah could've known that much about buildin ships unless an expert told him how. I think that expert was none other than God. Now let's get over to the school house cause even though it's Sunday I need you to help clean up."

There was only one week left of the school year and this made me happy because I was looking forward to finishing the sixth grade. Mom and Dad were also happier than usual. They had enjoyed knowing the people of Republican and appreciated their hospitality but they were

BORROWED BIBLES

looking forward to owning their own property again. And the next Saturday evening after supper, Dad made the announcement that he had bought a farm not too far away in an area east of Conway called Liberty and we would be moving there in a few weeks. Over the past year we had sold a lot of our furniture stored in a bedroom and the barn and Dad said that what was left of our excess furniture had just been sold to some newlyweds. So, unlike our move to Republican from Oregon, only a regular sized truck that would fit on the local bridges would be needed to move us to Liberty.

Joan was heartbroken over the news since it meant she would have to say good-bye to Max but they did promise to write to each other forever. She finally got up enough courage, though, to ask if Max could come to the house, take her for a walk and give her a chance to say a final good bye. Normally, Mom and Dad wouldn't have agreed because they thought at 15 Joan was too young to go for a walk with a boy. But to console her they agreed but they put several conditions on Max's visit. First, this was to be the last meeting with Max. He was to arrive at 7:00 p.m. on the coming Friday and they were to return to the house no later than 8:30 p.m. They were to walk only to the general store, buy something if they wanted, and sit on one of the benches in front of the store in full public sight. Finally, I was to go with them, walk behind and report to Mom and Dad if anything got out of line between them. When Joan heard the last condition, she turned to me with a look of anger and disgust but she accepted the conditions and then stormed into the bedroom to be alone.

Max arrived promptly at 7:00 p.m.; Dad shook his hand, and directed him to an empty chair in the living room. Max's chair faced a couch where Dad, Mom Joan and I were sitting and he looked as if he was facing a jury and in a way he was. I was so used to seeing Joan in everyday clothes that I was surprised how pretty she looked wearing her new dress she made especially for the occasion. And I saw her discreetly give Max a wave, which relaxed him a bit. Max, on the other hand, wore the same overalls and blue shirt that he always wore to church and school.

Mom and I didn't talk and after saying, "Pleased to meet you," to each of us, Max didn't say anything either; however, Dad did. He told Max that this was Joan's first date and that there better not be any funny business. He was expected to bring Joan back no later than 8:30 and at that time he, Max, was expected to go home. Then, Dad told Max and Joan they could leave, but I was to walk behind them at all times and for us to have a good time.

I was very embarrassed walking behind Joan and wished my parents hadn't made me do it. Max and Joan gave me angry looks but didn't say a word to me. They walked very close together and talked very quietly. I purposely stayed far enough behind so that I couldn't hear what they said. I figured that at least I could give them that little bit of privacy. Although we quarreled a lot, and got each other in trouble at times, I decided to not give Joan any trouble on her first date.

At one point Max reached out for Joan's hand but she didn't take it. I wondered if she would have if I hadn't been looking.

It didn't take long for us to pass by the public well and from there I could see that the blacksmith shop was closed, but the general store was open and the benches in front were fortunately vacant. I also heard someone in the church playing the piano. I hoped that it wasn't Reverend Knox whom I didn't want to run into. I was concerned that we might see him because he often showed up at the church or the general store at all kinds of hours. And he loved playing the church piano.

Max and Joan went into the general store while I waited outside but they soon returned and sat on a bench in front of the store as Dad had ordered. Max had bought them each a soft drink and a cupcake, the chocolate kind with a creamy center. I sat on a hitching post close to the blacksmith shop because from there I had a good view of the bench without being too close. I made sure not to stare at them but from time to time I looked in their direction. Max and Joan seemed to be having a good time. They were laughing a lot and several times Joan gave him a playful punch on the shoulder. When Max got up to return the empty soft drink bottles, I knew it was about time to leave.

As we walked back to our house, Max reached out for Joan's hand again and this time she took it and they slowed down to make their walk last as long as they could. When they got to the front door, they held both hands for a moment and then rapidly kissed. I stayed and watched from the road in front of our house, a good distance from them. Max left and passed by me on his way home. He had his fists clenched, and still didn't say a word to me but he did give me a long, dirty look. Joan waited for me at the front door and when I got there, she said, "Well, I hope you got your eyes full!"

"I'm not gonna say anything," I replied. We both entered the house. Joan was crying loudly and rushed to our bedroom without speaking to Mom or Dad.

Dad was puzzled and said, "What's wrong with her? We let her out for over an hour! You'd think she'd be happy."

Mom added, "And she got to wear her new dress too. Well, she's hard to figure out sometimes."

Then Dad turned to me and asked, "Did they behave?"

"Everything was OK," I said.

On my last Sunday in Republican, I finished reading Genesis and read Exodus, the second book of the Old Testament, through Chapter 20 where God gave Moses the Ten Commandments. It seemed that everyone I knew had heard of the Commandments; they were even more famous than Noah's Ark, and they were another part of the Old Testament that Dad said was true and important. My Sunday school teachers had mentioned them many times, Reverend Knox had referred to them in some of his sermons and my schoolteachers had also referred to them. Yet, it wasn't until that last Sunday in Republican that I concentrated on them as I read them to myself. I thought I knew them very well but the second Commandment puzzled me. I reread it several times because it seemed so strange and scary. To me, it meant that God got jealous if people worshiped anything other than Him and He would not only punish the person that worshiped the wrong way but also the children of that person all the way through the third and fourth generations. So according to this Commandment, if my great-grandfather had worshiped the wrong way, he would be punished, but I would be punished too even though I hadn't done anything wrong. And there was nothing I could do about it. Nothing! Surely, my understanding couldn't be true. I asked Mom and Dad about it but they both said they had never thought much about it and it was just one of those Bible mysteries that they didn't worry about. They said I shouldn't worry about it either.

I had already written in my notebook about being puzzled why God instructed Joshua to not only kill but also how to kill—even after

QUESTIONS

issuing the Sixth Commandment to not kill. I made another entry about being puzzled by the Second Commandment. Then, feeling discouraged again, I closed my Bible and notebook.

[Courtesy Faulkner County Arkansas Museum]

The Republican, Arkansas Blacksmith Shop

Although this photo was probably taken sometime in the 1930s, the building looked the same when I lived in Republican in 1946-47. I boarded the "chicken coop" to Conway in front of this shop. And it is from this shop that I watched Joan and Max talk in front of the general store only a few yards away to the left.

CHAPTER 7

Confrontations

WE MOVED TO our farm in Liberty, Arkansas in June 1947 and stayed for only about six months, a short period of time even for us. But some major events happened during that time. I finished reading the Old Testament; I learned how to plow with our mare, Bird, and Joan and I learned sign language so we could send messages back and forth without making noise and without anyone else understanding them. We also got a new dog that I named Lady. Joan and I both owned her but in a short period of time Lady really became just my dog since I was the only one who fed or played with her.

Joan and I were given the choice of attending Liberty School, a few miles west of our farm and closer to Conway, or Vilonia School a few miles east of our farm. To help us choose, we were invited to visit each school for a day to see which one we liked the best. We chose to visit Vilonia first and my day went very well visiting the seventh grade class until recess but then it took a bad and strange turn. I was standing in line to be a batter in a baseball game when a boy came up behind me holding a baseball bat. I thought he was just waiting his turn to be a batter but he swung his bat as if he were trying to hit a home run and hit me on purpose across the middle of my back as he yelled, "And I hit you on the back, choo!" He kept yelling "choo!" as I rolled around on the ground with severe pain. A couple of teachers who were supervising the play grounds hurried over and led him away while another teacher leaned over and told me softly but firmly to stop rolling around since that would make me worse. It didn't take long for someone who knew first aid to come and look me over. After poking my back in several places, the first aid person decided I didn't have any broken bones and it would be all right for me to move. I was helped to my feet and supported on each side while I walked, painfully, inside to the teachers' lounge where I was led to a large chair. I stayed in the teachers' lounge the rest of the day and from time to time someone would come and check on me. As to why that boy hit me and as to why he yelled, "choo," the answer I got was he hit me because he really didn't like strangers very much but he really liked the sound of "choo" so he went around saying it a lot. Fortunately, he hit me on a Friday and I had the weekend to recover before my scheduled visit to Liberty School on the coming Monday. In my parents' mind, the baseball bat attack determined that Vilonia School was out of the question and Joan and I would attend Liberty School. Joan had liked her visit to Vilonia very much and wanted to go there. But for once Dad didn't let her get her way. He said that he couldn't trust a school that would allow a crazy kid to roam around on the playground and hit other kids with a baseball bat. And there was no doubt the kid was crazy because no one in their right mind goes around yelling "choo." This made Joan real mad and although deep in her heart I don't think she blamed me, she punched me when she got the chance anyway.

I attended the seventh grade at Liberty School for several weeks before we moved again; the school itself was a bland experience with no notable memories. What was remarkable, however, was the joy I had after school when I harnessed Bird, hooked her up to a plow and spent an hour or so plowing our fields. It was very satisfying to see the plow turn over the weed-covered old dirt and expose new soil that would soon be planted with corn, peanuts and watermelons. School was over in the late afternoon so it was not too hot when I started plowing and as a special pleasure sometimes a breeze would come up that carried with it the refreshing smell of good, fresh dirt. And plowing all by myself made me feel important because I took it to mean that Mom and Dad thought I was beginning to be grown up. Bird was a very experienced mare and always obeyed the commands I spoke to her or sent her by tugging on her reins. It was a good thing she was experienced because a couple of times I was so startled by a quail flying out of the weeds that I yelled and jumped a couple of feet. Fortunately, Bird wasn't startled at all or she might have bolted and run away pulling the plow and me with her. Instead, she calmly shook her head and continued pulling the plow as if nothing had happened. Usually, Bird's mule colt, Red, would trot alongside us as she pulled the plow. Red was a very handsome, healthy mule, tarnished copper in color like his mother, and with a mischievous glint in his eyes. He was good company, fun to be with and fun to watch. Moreover, he never wandered very far even though I didn't use any harness to keep him in place. Oh, sometimes he would gallop a few yards away, snort and fool around a bit but he always came back real soon to be along side his mother. Once, I decided to leave him in his stall while I plowed with Bird but that didn't work out very well. After I had plowed for a few minutes, I heard a loud braying coming from the barn and the troubling sounds of Red trying to kick down the sides of the barn. I hurried back, opened his stall and he leaped out. He ran directly to where we had been plowing, bucked and snorted a couple of times and from then on trotted happily at Bird's side. Sometimes Lady would join us and walk next to Red but she got bored easily and never stayed with us very long. She preferred to run around and sniff at trees and briar patches hoping to flush some critter out in the open—I think a rabbit was what she hoped for most.

Bird was an excellent plow horse and also an expert at keeping me from riding her. Several times I took her from her stall and tried to climb on her back and ride bareback but every time, except once, she moved exactly at the last moment and kept me off. The one time I was able to get on her back, I regretted it because she alternated between raring up and refusing to move at all. Then she turned her head around and looked me directly in the eye as if to ask, "Have you had enough?" Yes, I had enough! Bird won! I was mad at her but at the same time admired her skill at keeping me off her back.

On most Sundays, Joan and I walked to Antioch Church located between our farm and Vilonia School. The church was only about two years old with a white front but with its sides and back still unpainted because of lack of money. And openings had been made for two windows on one side but again because of lack of money the openings had been boarded up. The church was built as a community project that began when the land plus a small amount of money for an initial building fund had been left in a local famer's will. Members of the community had donated additional money and volunteered materials and labor for its construction but there weren't enough resources to finish the church. There was also no formal affiliation with any national church and there was a dispute among the members what denomination the church should be. In the meantime, an uneasy agreement was reached that it was "sort of a Baptist church" as Mom and Dad called it. There was no paid preacher but several men of the community who knew a lot about the Bible agreed to be unpaid, temporary preachers for about three months each. Dad was asked to be one of the temporary preachers but he declined with thanks because he was busy on Sundays doing his college homework. It was believed that with the on-going fund raising programs, there would eventually be enough money to pay a full-time preacher and finish the construction of the church. In the meantime, it was an enjoyable church to go to and since it was new and unpainted, there was a pleasant smell of lumber inside. Everyone was very friendly and went out of their way to make Joan and me welcome because we were about the only kids that attended. The adults enjoyed talking to me because they were very intrigued with my plans that I made at such a young age to be a preacher and with my knowledge of the Old Testament. It was during these talks at church that I learned the residents around the Liberty area had developed colorful and useful words that I never heard anywhere else inside or outside of Arkansas. One word was "shoot-a-me-knows" that meant about the same as "gosh" or "you don't say." And it was usually said with an exclamation; for example, one person might say "I caught ten fish today" and the response might be, "Well, shoot-a-me-knows!" Another word was "goody-ill" a very useful word that was used to negate the comments said by another person or a question asked by another person. For example, if I told someone "It looks like rain today," they might disagree by saying "goody-ill." Or if I asked, "Are you going to Conway tomorrow?" they might tell me they weren't going by saying, "goody-ill." Our family immediately liked these words a lot and we made them a permanent part of our vocabulary.

 Joan and I would sit as far apart as we could in church while still being able to see each other so we could enjoy the sneaky kind of fun of sending messages with sign language. We seldom had the chance to send a complete word without an adult seeing us but we could usually send a letter of the sign language alphabet so we came up with a code using one letter only. The three we used most often were, "L" for "laughing," "B" for "boring" and "H" for "hungry." Joan didn't enjoy church nearly as much as I did so she sent me the "B" signal a lot but I usually sent her the "H" signal.

Brother Carl Baker was the volunteer preacher when we first started going to Antioch. He said that during his three months of preaching he was going to say a lot about the apostle Paul because, "Next to Jesus, Paul's the most important person in Christianity. He wrote 13 New Testament books—that's how important he is!" Brother Baker went on to tell us that Paul didn't start life as a Christian but as a Jew and Roman citizen known as Saul. At one time he even persecuted the followers of Jesus and played a part in having them arrested for heresy. But he had a life changing experience, came to accept Jesus as the Son of God, was baptized and changed his name to Paul. Then he traveled from country to country, established congregations and performed miracles. Paul claimed that God spoke to him directly and told him to spread the word that it was no longer required for males to be circumcised nor for converts to obey the Jewish dietary laws. He said the only thing required to get into heaven was to accept Jesus.

For the next several Sundays, Brother Baker based his sermons on the 13 New Testament books that Paul wrote while in prison for blasphemy. The sermons about Paul helped me understand things a lot better. I had just finished reading the Old Testament and remembered that God told Abraham that all male babies should be circumcised when they were eight days old—but I hadn't been circumcised. And God named lots of food that we weren't supposed to eat—but we had been eating the forbidden food anyway. Dad had said that there were laws in the Old Testament that we didn't have to obey anymore but he never explained why. But Brother Baker's sermons did explain why. It was because Jesus had died for our sins, Paul had accepted Jesus as the Son of God; God changed some of the laws in the Old Testament and told Jesus about the changes; Jesus then told Paul about the changes and then told Paul to spread the word throughout the land.

A few weeks before we moved from our Liberty farm, Bill left Portland, moved in with us and shared a bedroom with me. He had wanted to experience living in Arkansas again and a serious quarrel with his girl friend in Portland gave him all the additional incentive he needed to move back with us. He was 23 years old and didn't have a job lined up in Arkansas but with his mechanical skills he was sure he would easily find one. He was right; after just a few days of looking, he got a good job as an automotive mechanic in nearby Conway.

We owned a 1935 Chevrolet Standard sedan, similar to the 1934 Chevrolet sedan we had owned years earlier at Steel Bridge just before we moved to Vancouver. When Bill arrived, the Chevy was barely running and there were lots of loose parts that rattled. Bill soon made the car much better. He tuned it up, replaced some parts, cleaned other parts and tightened everything that was loose. I helped out a bit by handing him wrenches and cleaning some of the car parts in coal oil. And by helping, I was learning to be a mechanic also and I really liked it. Bill also took over some of the plowing duties but that meant I reluctantly had to share the enjoyable times I spent with Bird. He was very good plowing with her but even though he had a lot more experience with horses than I did, he was never able to climb on her back and ride her either.

For all practical purposes, there were no zoning laws for Liberty so just about any kind of business could be started very easily. Mr. Gemmil, the farmer who lived next door, decided to get into the used car business and he was able to do it in just a few hours. He parked three cars in his front yard right next to the road to Conway and put big "For Sale" signs on them. He also strung a rope between two poles with colored pieces of cloth hanging on it. They flapped really good in the breeze and helped bring attention to the cars.

Mr. Gemmil had a son, Hank, about my age and we sometimes played together. After the car business was started, I spent a lot more time visiting Hank because I really liked exploring the cars for sale. At first, there were three: a 1929 Ford Model A Business Coupe with a rumble seat, a 1936 Ford sedan and a 1938 Buick sedan. My favorite was the Buick because the inside was so fancy, big and interesting. I thought only rich people owned Buicks so I asked Hank where his father got it but he said his father wouldn't tell him. And when I asked Mr. Gemmil directly, he said it was a, "car dealer's secret." The Buick's headlights with four levels of brightness especially fascinated me: there was city-bright, city-dim, country-bright and country-dim. Hank and I would sit inside and take turns in the driver's seat. We would pretend we were going on a long trip and we'd describe the scenery as we drove up imaginary steep, mountains and across long, imaginary bridges.

CONFRONTATIONS

And we would honk the horn and turn on the headlights making sure we used all four levels of brightness. One day we ran the battery down so low with our imaginary driving that the Buick wouldn't start. Mr. Gemmil came outside, made us get out of the car and made us promise never to use the horn or lights again or we would never be allowed inside any of the cars again. We kept our promise too because we sure didn't want to give up our imaginary trips.

One day I walked over to see Hank and straight away noticed the Buick wasn't there. A 1938 Pontiac sedan was parked in its place instead. Hank said his Dad traded cars the day before and was very happy about it since he made a lot of money by doing the trade. That made me sad because I hoped somehow we would find a way to buy the Buick and that I'd learn how to drive it. The Pontiac, while not as impressive as the Buick, was still very good looking with its shiny black paint job, a little red trim here and there and its distinctive Indian hood ornament. Mr. Gemmil told me he was going to talk to my dad about trading cars because he was in the mood to give a real good deal if Dad would trade our Chevy for the Pontiac. The next day Mr. Gemmil walked over to our farm and invited Dad to, "Come over and look at a '38 Pontiac I just took in. Right now I can make you a world beatin deal on a trade. I guarantee—you won't be sorry!"

Dad asked Bill to go with him because he wanted an expert mechanic's opinion about the car. Bill happily agreed and grabbed an old quilt so he would have something to lie on when he rolled under the car to inspect it. I was allowed to tag along but told to stay out of the way and to be quiet. While we were walking over to see the Pontiac, Bill cautioned Dad that Mr. Gemmil struck him as a real wheeler-dealer so as a bargaining strategy he suggested that Dad shouldn't show much interest but act disappointed no matter how he really felt. Dad agreed, so he just slowly walked around the Pontiac and didn't say a word, but whenever he saw the slightest scratch he would rub it and shake his head disapprovingly. Dad asked for the Pontiac's previous owner's name so we could talk to him and find out why he wanted to get rid of it. Mr. Gimmel told him that was a car dealer's secret but he assured Dad not to worry because the previous owner was a God-fearing Christian that loved nothing better than taking good care of cars.

Meanwhile, Bill had opened the hood, tugged on wires, unscrewed the radiator cap and looked in the radiator and unscrewed the air filter cover and looked in the carburetor. Then, he put the quilt on the ground, got on it, rolled under the car and grabbed parts of the front-end suspension and shook them. After he got back up, he pushed down on the front and rear bumpers to test the suspension. He joined Dad in pretending to be disappointed by the way the car had checked out but I could tell from the way he squinted his eyes that he really liked it. After tinkering with one of the door latches that needed tightening, Bill asked, "Well, does it start and run good?"

Mr. Gemmil pretended to be surprised and hurt by the question but replied, "You bet it runs good! Better than a sewing machine! Go ahead and start her up. She'll start real good too."

Bill got behind the steering wheel, started the engine and said it didn't turn over nearly as fast as it should.

"No sir, it turned over just fine. That's the way a Pontiac is—slow but sure." Mr. Gemmil said with a knowledgeable tone.

Bill revved the engine and listened carefully. He pulled out the choke and gave a look of disgust when the choke had no effect. Then he stepped on the brakes and said they were too soft and he turned the steering wheel back and forth and said it had too much play.

"Lots of things wrong," Bill said, "But we'd like to take it for a short drive anyway. OK?"

Mr. Gemmil said it was more than OK because that's the best way to appreciate how fine a car a Pontiac is. And then he asked Dad if he could borrow the keys to Dad's Chevy. He thought it would be a good idea for him to walk over to our farm and take a look at the Chevy while we were test-driving the Pontiac.

Dad agreed and loaned him the keys.

Hank said he wanted to come with us but Mr. Gemmil told him he couldn't. "We'll let the Goods go by themselves so they can talk about the Pontiac in private."

Bill scooted over to the passenger's seat while Dad got behind the wheel and I sat in the back seat. As soon as Dad shifted into low and let out the clutch, the engine died. Dad said, "It's more high-strung than our Chevy." He restarted it and tried again. This time the Pontiac

CONFRONTATIONS

moved with a slow, jerky pace out to the road. We headed east toward Vilonia.

Dad was smiling when the speedometer got up to 50 and his smile was even bigger when it got up to 60. "Most powerful car I've ever driven!" he said. He tried the horn, wipers and lights and asked Bill to open the glove compartment and take a look—it was empty. Dad said to Bill, "I like it but I could see you found a lot wrong and aren't happy with it."

Bill answered, "There's a lot wrong but nothing serious. Things like the door handle can be fixed easy and so can the wiring. The underneath looks pretty good and I didn't see any big oil leaks. It needs a new tire but we can get one cheap. I like it but I didn't want him to see that I like it. That way you can bargain with him better. It'd help though if I drove it back when you turn around."

Dad agreed and when we got to Vilonia, he stopped the car and changed positions. Bill drove back to Mr. Gemmil's farm while he and Dad discussed whether or not to buy the car. Dad said he probably would because he was going to interview for a real good teaching job in Paron that he had just heard about. And it would be more impressive to go to the interview in a fancy car like the Pontiac instead of a common Chevy.

Bill said that he had never heard of Paron and wanted to know where it was and how far away it was.

Dad answered, "About 60 miles—it's over in Saline County not far from Benton. I never heard of it before either but they've got two great teachin jobs open and your Mom and I are gonna drive over and interview for them."

When we returned, Mr. Gemmil was outside waiting for us with his arms crossed and with a big grin on his face. It was clear that he wanted the first word so he rushed up to Dad and said, "I looked at your Chevy and I like it! So here's the deal." He went on to tell Dad how much money he'd have to add to the Chevy to own the Pontiac and Dad didn't show any expression at all but said, "Too much! Knock $50 off and I'll think about it." Mr. Gemmil got mad and said there was nothing to think about because there wasn't a chance in hell he'd take that "highway robbery" kind of a deal. And he said it was his suppertime, anyway, so he left us and went to eat. Dad, Bill and I walked back to our farm.

That evening Dad was pretty sad because he really liked the Pontiac and he told us at the supper table that maybe he should have taken the deal because it actually seemed pretty good. He said he'd sleep on it and maybe walk over the next morning and tell Mr. Gemmil he'd take the deal after all. Mom shook her head "no" and said we didn't need to waste money by trading cars—instead we should be buying new clothes. But Bill told Dad he should take the deal because he had done all he could do repairing the Chevy and it wasn't going to last much longer.

After breakfast, Dad got his checkbook and stuffed it in his rear pocket and told Mom he was going to walk over to Gemmil's place and buy the Pontiac and there wasn't anything she could do to stop him. She didn't say anything but did give him a dirty look. And she wasn't happy with Bill either because he had taken Dad's side. But before Dad could open the front door, Mr. Gemmil drove in our front yard honking the horn of the Pontiac as he drove. Dad grinned and hurried out the front door to meet him. We watched what was happening between the two men and saw lots of hand shaking, backslapping and laughing. Then, Mr. Gemmil handed Dad some papers, Dad handed him a check and the keys to the Chevy and Mr. Gemmil drove it away. Dad hurried back to our house with the Pontiac now sitting prominently in our front yard. He held up the keys to the Pontiac and happily announced. "It's our car now! It's ours! He took my deal! Yes Sir, Suzy's ours now!" Mom asked with a suspicious tone, "And where'd you get that name of Suzy?" Dad told her that was a secret.

Mom hadn't been employed since she quit her job at Sears in Portland before we moved back to Arkansas. She got restless staying at home and felt a bit useless since Joan and I didn't need much care anymore. And she missed having money of her own. So she was happy when Dad told her that the school in Paron needed a teacher for the commercial subjects that he taught; typing, shorthand and bookkeeping but they also needed a third grade teacher as well. Dad knew he was qualified for the commercial position because he was a high school graduate as well as a graduate of the Chillicothe Business College in Missouri and had taught those subjects before. In contrast, Mom had never taught school on a full time basis and had only completed the fourth grade. She partly educated herself, however, by reading everything she could and by playing elaborate spelling games whenever she could find a partner. And she was so good at explaining things to children that she had been a paid tutor and a substitute teacher for a few days in some communities where she had lived. Dad convinced her to create a resume and go with him to interview for the third grade teaching position when he went to interview for the commercial teaching position. Although she was nervous about doing it, she and Dad did create a resume for her and she went for the interview. The Paron semester had already started and the school administrators were desperate to have the positions filled. Dad and Mom were impressive appearing people; they had persuasive, albeit partly fictional, resumes and they came across as first-rate teachers at their interviews in Paron. They were both offered the teaching jobs on the spot without their references checked but with one condition—they had to start teaching in one week. They accepted the condition.

Mom and Dad were happy when they returned from Paron about their new jobs but very unhappy with Suzy. In fact, Dad was more than unhappy—he was mad because Suzy had boiled over four times on their round trip and one time she did it where the closest water was a few miles away. He had to make a long walk to a farm and pay a farmer for a couple of gallons of water for the radiator. Meanwhile, Mom waited in the car and that made her nervous because she was afraid someone would see that she was stranded and stop, rob her, torture her and then slowly kill her. Up to that time, Dad made excuses when Suzy boiled over but when it happened at such an inconvenient location, and he had to walk a long way and then pay for the water on top of it—well, that was the last straw. He was also mad at Bill because Bill had looked Suzy over and didn't find any problems and that was one of the reasons Dad had bought her. Bill was surprised too so he checked Suzy again and said that a small crack had developed in her bottom radiator hose and cracks like that couldn't be predicted. He replaced the radiator hose and told Dad and Mom that Suzy's problem hadn't been serious but in any case her problem was solved.

There were an endless number of things to do in order to start school in Paron in just one week. Dad immediately put our farm up for sale and was pretty sure it would be a quick sale but even so it would probably stand vacant for a while. Bill located a moving company in Conway who agreed to move the small amount of furniture we had at a bargain price and they also agreed to haul Bird and Red to the weekly Conway auction. My happy times with Bird and Red came to an end because there was no need for them or room for them in Paron. It was a sad day when I went with Dad to see them sold at the auction. The auctioneer said that Red would bring a good price because he was a fine young mule and would be real good at pulling a plow someday. But Bird was old, over the hill, and not worth much. She would be sent to a slaughterhouse and turned into cat food.

Bill said he wouldn't move with us to Paron because there wasn't anything for him to do there. And his job in Conway as a mechanic was going very well so he rented a small room close to his work place. He also bought a 1938 Chevrolet Coupe that he was very fond of and he constantly fine-tuned its carburetor and tinkered with its electrical system. It had taken him a long time to find a car that he liked as well as the '38 DeSoto he owned in Portland but the '38 Chevy was that car. With Bill leaving, Joan and I were, once again, the only two kids left at home.

I had been attending Liberty school for only a short time so entry into Paron School would make two schools in one year. In general I started to a new school every year because of our moves and the move to Paron would make the eighth school I attended in seven years. I never got used to being the "new kid" at school and I really dreaded it. There was an advantage to moving so often, however. Although I didn't really feel at home anywhere, I developed a quiet confidence that I would be able to cope anywhere.

The four of us stayed out of the way and waited inside Suzy with the windows rolled down while the moving truck was loaded. It didn't take long for the movers to pack and move our belongings to the truck and then they drove away. Mom told Joan and me to stay in the car while she and Dad walked through the house and checked to make sure that nothing was forgotten and that all the windows were locked. While they were in the house, Lady came out from under the house where she had been hiding, walked slowly over to our car, stood outside my door, looked sadly at me and wagged her tail. She sensed something was very wrong and looked at me for reassurance. I regretted that I couldn't give her reassurance and I wasn't able to look her in the eye. I knew that in just a little while Mom and Dad would return and we'd drive away and leave her. I had been told once again that there wasn't room to take a dog with us and there was an additional reason that we couldn't take Lady—Mom said she was going to have puppies. I was told not to worry though because the father of the puppies was a dog that lived on a farm up the road and the people who owned that farm really liked dogs and were sure to take care of Lady and her puppies. I reached a new depth of sadness by looking at Lady and thinking of leaving her behind. In addition to my immediate sadness caused by Lady, memories of my other dogs, Charlie and Penny and Fanny, flashed through my mind. I promised myself to never own another dog. It was too painful to leave them behind when we moved. It wasn't worth it.

We were very quiet during our drive to our new home in Paron. Each of us was hoping someone else would say something but none of us did. Mom's initial excitement about getting her first full time teaching job was replaced with fear that she would fail. Dad was worried about leaving our farm, empty and unsold. And although his salary at Paron was a good one, he had taken an immediate dislike to the superintendent and dreaded working for him. Both Joan and I were quietly dreading being the new kids at Paron and I was feeling extra-sorry for myself because I had been at Liberty such a short time that I still felt like the new kid there. Then, too, Joan and I didn't enjoy annoying each other like we used to so we paid more attention to our own thoughts. We were getting older and our relationship had changed quite a bit. Joan was much more interested in boys and spent a lot of time still thinking about Max in Republican. And she had met another boy at Liberty that she liked as much as Max. She sat next to me, thinking quietly about the boys and looking out the window, detached and unfocused. She ignored me and everything else. I was worried and lonely. I would have felt even lonelier if I hadn't known that Jesus was looking down at me and helping me in ways that I couldn't understand. I imagined Jesus sitting on a big, golden throne next to God who was sitting on another golden throne that was even bigger. Their thrones were in the clouds but not ordinary clouds like the ones we see from earth but special clouds, beautiful beyond description. And there they sat, God and Jesus, talking about the problems of the world and I figured that since I had accepted Jesus as a savior they would include my problems in their talks. I thought about how lucky I was because even though Jesus had lots of things to do, he still had enough time to pay attention to me and to look out for me. Mrs. Babcock, my Sunday school teacher in Portland, had been right. Jesus proved to be a true friend that I could always depend on no matter where I was, and no matter where we moved.

Water drops started to fall on Suzy's front windshield. I thought it was raining but the water was soon joined by steam coming from the engine and then we knew. Suzy was boiling over again. At first, Dad tried to ignore the steam hoping it would go away but it got thicker and then there was a loud hissing noise and the engine started shaking and knocking. Dad pulled onto the shoulder and turned the ignition off but the engine was so hot that it kept running for a while anyway. "Damn!" He said, "I thought Bill had fixed her." Ironically, where we stopped was close to where Suzy had boiled over when Mom and Dad had driven to Paron for interviews. This time, though, Dad was prepared. He waited for the engine to cool down, and then took water he had stored in Suzy's trunk and refilled the radiator. When he got back in the car, he said, "That radiator hose Bill put on still looks good so there's gottta be some other reason she boiled over. But we'll be able to make it to Paron now. Damn! I wish I'd never bought this car!"

Mom said with a satisfied voice, "Well, I told you not to. Didn't I?"

Paron was very different from all the other places we had lived and even different from any place we had heard of for that matter. The eight months I lived there was at the time, and still is today, the worst of my life. The harassment that I received there sent me into a deep stupor that was virtually a catatonic state and caused me to drop out of school without finishing the seventh grade. Although larger than Republican or Liberty, the community was more remote in a real sense because the people had become insular and unusually hostile to outsiders. That was bad for us because not only were we outsiders but also the "teacher family" so we were looked at with extra suspicion and unfriendliness. And somehow, the word had spread that we used to live in Oregon and to the locals that meant we had lived among black folks and had gone to school and church with them and that meant we were as bad as Yankees. Then, too, the locals had decided that since we had lived in "Yankee land," we were uppity and had lots of other undesirable (although unspecified) Yankee habits and we were treated very much like Yankees would have been treated. It wasn't just the people—even the trees seemed hostile. There were lots of them too. They were tall, grew jungle-like and seemed to lunge at me when I walked close to them. And they were full of ticks and caterpillars. The other places we had lived in Arkansas also had ticks but the trees, bushes and tall grass at Paron were overflowing with them and the short grass was overflowing with chiggers. I soon learned to walk in the middle of a road or path whenever I could; otherwise, I would be bitten by something. When I couldn't avoid foliage, I searched myself as soon as I got home and I would ask someone to search my scalp. More often than not, a tick about the size of a pencil eraser would be found on my body and more often than not I would suffer chigger bites anyway because the chiggers were too small to find. Many people living in Paron had been bitten by ticks and some had developed tick fever sometime in their lives. It was a bad experience they never forgot. The man who lived next door to us, Mr. Smetna, was without legs from his knees down. They had been amputated because of a severe infection caused, it was thought, by a tick bite. He moved around by sitting on a homemade wagon that he propelled by using his hands to push along the ground. He wore heavy gloves that helped prevent cuts and blisters and I only saw him once without his gloves.

    The kids at school avoided becoming friends with Joan and me but did enjoy making us the subjects of insults and pranks. We received several anonymous notes at school telling us how unwelcome we were. There was no relief outside of school either. We received anonymous letters at home with advertisements for guns and one letter had a drawing of a hangman's noose. We were told to stay inside our house, not to attend church, go to parties or attempt to visit anyone. When I went to the grocery store, the people who worked there went out of their way to make shopping unpleasant by ignoring me or telling me that they were out of whatever I wanted even when it could be clearly seen on the shelf. We learned to stock up on groceries from a store in

Benton, a small town about twenty miles away, so we could avoid the Paron store entirely.

The house we rented was only about fifty yards from the schoolyard so it was easy for the other kids to walk from school and sabotage it. It was common to have garbage dumped in our yard and Suzy was a very tempting target. Several times her spark plug wires were disconnected, and air was let out of her tires. Curiously and fortunately, no one broke any of her windows, stole her tires or any other parts. Dad started parking Suzy by the side of our house just outside a bedroom window and he spread the word that he had a rifle and wouldn't mind using it. These steps slowed down the sabotage to our property but didn't stop it entirely. The weekend brought a little relief but sometimes a car would slow down ominously in front of our house at night and its spotlight beam played on our windows. Then, with a blaring horn and racing motor the car would move away, flinging gravel from the road as it accelerated into the dark. It was a country version of burning rubber.

Sunday was the most restful day. We didn't attend church because we weren't welcome and anyway Mom and Dad were both taking correspondence courses from the Arkansas State Teachers College in Conway so they did homework together and that took up most of Saturday and Sunday. Their studies were interesting to me because they would talk about their assignments and I overheard some of it and learned some things. It was also interesting because they had just bought a new type of device to write with, a ballpoint pen, that we thought was amazing. Previously, they did their homework with a fountain pen and it was a lot of trouble to keep the pens filled and the ink from smearing. It was a major step when the administrators at the college decided, after quite a bit of deliberation, it would be acceptable to turn in homework done with ballpoint pens. They were expensive, though, so they weren't used for rough drafts but only for final homework. And too often, their ink would stop flowing—usually at inconvenient times; however, Mom and Dad soon learned tricks to get the ink flowing again. If they completed their homework in time on Sunday, we were allowed to listen to the radio starting at 6:00 p.m. for two hours assuming that nothing scandalous was being talked about. Once we were listening to the Phil Harris show when Phil's wife, Alice, said she thought she was pregnant. Abruptly, Dad leaped

CONFRONTATIONS

from his chair, turned the radio off and sent Joan and me to bed. When I got into bed, I could hear him still him complaining to Mom about how awful it was for "that show" to talk about pregnancy—especially on a Sunday because Sunday was God's special day. It was a long time before we were allowed to listen to the Phil Harris show again and I was really puzzled because I didn't know what "pregnant" meant until I was able to get Joan to tell me later.

One Sunday Dad told us that since we weren't welcome at church he was going to conduct services in the back yard like he used to do. So we moved some chairs to the back yard for Mom, Joan and me to sit on while Dad stood in front with his open Bible that he read a few passages from. Then he passed out the Bibles and hymnbooks he had taken from church and we sang a couple of songs ending with *The Old Rugged Cross* as usual. It seemed to me that Dad held this service only because he thought he should but his heart didn't seem to be in it. His reading and singing was flat and he didn't add his own thoughts to the readings like he used to. And he didn't say anything about the Church of Christ. The service didn't last very long and when it was over Dad said to me, "Some day, when you're a preacher, you'll be the one leadin the service." Then, he and Mom walked back into the house and continued doing their homework. Dad never conducted another church service.

On some Saturday mornings, Mom and Dad didn't do home work. Dad would put on his suit and tie, put lots of water in Suzy's trunk for the inevitable boil-overs, and head off early to Conway all by himself. He would spend most of the day in Conway looking for a house for us to move to just as soon as the Paron school year was over. And since it was so close to Conway, he would also go check on our farmhouse in Liberty that was still for sale and vacant. Mom hinted that it would be nice if he took her "and the kids" with him some of the time but he said he could save money by going by himself and he could look at more houses by being alone too. We were all so eager to leave Paron that we waited for him to come back in the evening with the same excitement we had waiting for Christmas morning. When he did come back, we would crowd around him hoping to hear good news. And one memorable Saturday he returned with a huge smile on his face saying he had closed the deal on a wonderful house on a paved street with running water, electricity, three bedrooms, with schools and a Church of Christ nearby and he said we were gonna love it!

A strange mental disorder afflicted several of the Paron families. There were people in their twenties severely retarded who were still attending school even though they could only grunt and couldn't find their way from one class room to another. Mom had one student, Bob, like that in her third grade class and there was another one, Hugh, who was in my seventh grade class. There were other students, all males, equally retarded in other classes. At the end of each class period, another student, usually a relative with normal abilities, would lead the retarded student to the next event, make sure they had food and water and take them to the outdoor toilets. At the end of the school day, they would be led to the school bus and someone would meet them at their bus stop and lead them home. They would be fed, their clothing attended to and, since physically they were young men, their beards would be shaved as needed and that was once a day in some cases. It was understood that these individuals would never pass since they didn't even understand what was being said in class. School served as a baby-sitter.

There was another student, Tom, in my class who was also retarded but not nearly to the extent as Hugh. He had passed his classes, but just barely, and he could take care of himself, but just barely. Tom had a severe ailment that caused his skin to be a yellowish color and there were large dark circles under his eyes. He was part of a family of fifteen children, primarily girls, because many of the boys died of the same, but unidentified, disease when they were about Tom's age. I had been attending Paron School for about a month when Tom died. His family was experienced in funeral arrangements and they moved rapidly to have a funeral service and burial two days after Tom's death. The family was very poor and couldn't afford an undertaker so he was not embalmed. They couldn't afford a professional casket either so his body was put in a simple homemade box made of rough pine lumber and placed for viewing in a large tent close to Paron School. The school superintendent dismissed all classes and we were told to attend the funeral services. Ordinarily, I wouldn't have been invited to the funeral and I didn't want to go but my homeroom teacher said I was expected to attend since Tom was a classmate. It was a short

CONFRONTATIONS

walk to the tent and as I walked to it I saw Dad, Mom and Joan also walking over with their respective groups. A large crowd had gathered inside the tent and that wasn't surprising since Tom had a lot of sisters, a few younger brothers, countless other relatives and virtually all of Paron School was in attendance. Some chairs had been brought to the tent for Tom's immediate family but most of the audience stood. The preacher's message was brief and was essentially that while it was easy and natural to think that Tom was too young to die, God had a special reason to bring him home to heaven years before his time; therefore, Tom was special. We were told to not be sad but to rejoice because Tom was in a better place and he could now visit with all his brothers that were already in heaven. Then, it was time to view Tom's body and we formed a long, single line that snaked around the tent. I didn't want to view his body—I had never seen a dead human and I definitely didn't want to see a dead classmate, but I moved through the line anyway. Since Tom hadn't been embalmed, his body experienced unpredictable movements as some of his organs expanded from heat and bacteria activity. Knowing this might happen, his family used a scarf to tie his lower jaw tight against the upper jaw so people wouldn't have to see his open mouth. Then, just before the viewing started, someone removed the scarf so Tom would look more natural. The plan was for Tom's jaw to remain closed after the scarf was removed. And it did—it did, that is, until it was my turn to view him. As bad luck would have it, Tom's mouth flew open the exact moment I looked into his casket. That vivid and frightening moment stayed with me for years and it reappeared often as part of a sweat-soaked nightmare. I abruptly stopped looking into the casket and moved to the back of the tent. No one came forward to re-tie Tom's scarf and the next person in line didn't move to look inside the casket either. There was a moment of embarrassed silence. Then, Tom's father walked up and solemnly nailed the lid to the casket. The viewing had come to a dramatic close.

Someone backed up a large, red Reo truck with a flat bed to the opening of the tent. Several men picked up Tom's casket, placed it on the truck bed, then sat next to it and held it down. The truck was well known in Paron because it was the only one with a double-low gear or "granny gear" as it was called. The driver used the granny gear to good effect to make the truck go extra-slow like a hearse and that added some dignity and solemnity as the truck drove off. The casket was transported to a grave that had been freshly dug on Tom's farm just a few feet away from the graves of four of his brothers. All had died at just about Tom's age and I was told that all the brothers had also developed yellowish skin with dark circles under their eyes a few weeks before they died.

There were four buildings on the Paron School campus. The main building housed the administrative offices, most of the classrooms, a library that doubled as a study hall and a cafeteria where students could eat their lunch they brought from home although most preferred to sit and eat on the playground. There were a few more classrooms in the gymnasium located about 50 yards from the main building and two large outdoor toilets at the back of the campus, one for girls and one for boys.

We would start the school day in our home room located in the main building, then every hour we would move to our next class and at the end of the school day we would return to our home room. I enjoyed the subject matter of the classes but wished they had been more challenging in an intellectual sense. The classes did present a big social challenge, however, because of the hostility of the other students toward me. There were two basic causes for the hostility: I was the "teacher's kid" of a teacher they didn't like and I was "that new kid from Oregon" and that made me a Yankee. The class I dreaded the most was the third period Civics class since to get to it, I had to walk over to a classroom in the gymnasium. The other students turned my walk into a long gauntlet of insults. They would line up next to the pathway and yell, "Hey teacher's pet! Think you're smart don't you? You like Niggers don't you? Hey Oregon! Why don't you go back to Oregon?" They would say, "Oregon," with foaming-at-the-mouth hatred and then spell it out like a football cheer, "O-R-E-G-O-N!" And it was worse when I got to the classroom because it was Dad who taught the class. He insisted on discipline and having things his way but the students didn't like his way and they didn't like him or me. There were fourteen students in Dad's class and this included only two other students that were "friendly" toward him; there was Hugh who was so retarded he didn't even understand where he was and there was Evelyn, the daughter of the Paron math teacher. Her father had directed her as a show of teacher solidarity to behave in Dad's class no matter what the other students did. The other eleven students took every opportunity to openly misbehave or to secretly give encouragement to the students that did misbehave. If Dad turned his back, then they would throw gravel or some type of rubbish trying to hit him on his rear end. When he tried to talk, several students would hum loudly trying to drown him out. He would try to figure out who had hummed but of course everyone denied doing it. Sooner or later, out of frustration, Dad would stride to an offending student's desk and if it were a boy, he would grab the student by the hair or shirt collar and forcibly march him to the hall. When Dad was in the hall, gravels and rubbish would be thrown at me. Girls were treated differently; they would be shouted at and told to leave the room. Fortunately, they always did because I don't know how Dad would have handled a girl if she had refused to move. As soon as Dad returned from the hall to resume teaching, another student would take over the job of disrupting the class and then that student would be expelled from the classroom too. It was not unusual for most of the class period to be taken up with Dad sending students from his classroom. Once the superintendent came into the classroom during the middle of one of these confrontations and told the students to behave and to obey Mr. Good. Out of respect for the superintendent the students became quiet and remained quiet for the rest of the period. The next day, however, the truce ended and the students resumed their troublemaking behavior. About the only time that the class behaved was when Dad gave a test on homework that had been assigned. He had learned that some of the students feared flunking more than they enjoyed misbehaving, so he started giving tests during the last half of every class period and he used the first half to go over material that might be on the test. Several weeks passed, however, and he hadn't returned any of the tests so the students didn't know what grades they had earned. When it came close to mid-term, the teachers were required to issue grades that, while not final, did show the students their status at that time. Evelyn and I received an A and Hugh didn't receive a grade (that was the understanding concerning the retarded students). Dad gave one or two Cs and gave Fs to the rest, flunking most of the class. Unfortunately, he had no documentation to substantiate his grades that were highly subjective. In fact, in his anger, Dad hadn't even graded the tests but based the grade he gave on how disruptive the student had been. The Civics grades from Dad were the match that ignited the explosion that had been building during the school year. All the students except for me, Evelyn and Hugh walked out of his class and never returned. And at class time they gathered outside the window of his class, shouted and sang songs. The superintendent talked to Dad about his grades but Dad refused to change them. And the superintendent talked to the boycotting students and asked them to return to class and to be quiet. They refused to return to class unless Dad changed the grades first but they did move away from his classroom window and to a more distant part of the playground.

The intensity of my harassment up to the time of the student boycott had been severe but it got worse afterward. Outside of class, one or more students would put their face a few inches from mine and shout cuss words at me until I reached the next class. And some students positioned themselves perfectly to spit on me. I quit going to the bathroom because there were always some boys close enough to come in after me, push me into a corner and punch me in the stomach—stomach punches wouldn't show like punches to the face would. Some of the teachers saw the punishment I was receiving and would sometimes come to my aid and make the other students leave me alone, but the relief was only temporary. The teachers couldn't protect me all the time. The harassment at the house got worse too. More students gathered outside our house before they boarded their buses to go home. They made more noise, and threw more rubbish. And on the weekend instead of an occasional single car that threatened us, there could be a convoy of cars and trucks that would slow down ominously in front of our house and dump garbage.

I tried to cope with the increased harassment by purposely arriving at school a few minutes after it started in order to avoid students whom I knew would be waiting for me. The superintendent agreed to move Dad's class to the main building where it would be more isolated from the boycotting students and I wouldn't have the gauntlet to run between the two buildings. But I made a huge and stupid mistake. I thought I could earn some sympathy from the students if they thought I didn't have very long to live. So, I told a student who I knew would spread the word that I had a fatal disease and only had a few weeks to live. My strategy backfired—someone composed a chant about how happy everyone would be after I died. I was soon taunted by the chant. It was sung to me throughout the day, and to make sure I received the message, an anonymous letter was sent to our house containing the words of the chant.

There was nowhere I could go to escape the harassment. It was severe at school but continued at our house. The weekends were filled with terror of a different kind but of similar degree. It was hard to sleep and there was always a knot in my stomach with occasional vomiting. Finally, there came a day at school when I could no longer cope. After I completed the first period class in my homeroom, I started to walk down the hall to my next class when I realized that nothing was in focus and my walk was wobbly. The students were yelling at me as usual. I could see fuzzy images of their lips moving, and I could hear the noise but I couldn't understand any of the words they were saying. I tried to scream out something in my defense but discovered that my voice didn't work and I couldn't say anything. I knew I wouldn't be able to make it back to our house, and then I decided that I would choose to die rather than go to another class. So I continued to stumble down the hallway, still not able to speak. I had a dim memory of one room that was seldom used that had a small closet inside. It was difficult but I found my way to that closet, let myself in and closed the door behind me. It was quiet inside and so dark that I couldn't see but that made it more appealing. I was comforted by the quiet and the dark and sat down in a corner. I planned to stay in the closet until school ended and then try to sneak home without being seen. I didn't know what was wrong with me but I thought a few hours of peace and quiet might help whatever it was.

I had been asleep for about an hour when the closet door opened. Miss Thurman, one of the teachers, smiled at me, held out her hand and said, "Come on, Lester, I'm gonna walk you home." She held my hand tight and walked me out of the school building. She had seen me enter the unused classroom and had wondered why I hadn't come out. She also knew the severe harassment I had been receiving and waited to check on me between classes when there wouldn't be other students in the hall. As we were walking on the road that led to our house, she spoke quietly, "I'd like to know how you're feeling. Tell me if you hurt anywhere." My lips moved but I wasn't able to speak. Instead, I stopped in the road, bent over and vomited a little bit. Miss Thurman squeezed my hand and said, "It's OK, don't worry about talking then. You'll be home soon and your parents and sister Joan will be home soon too." Fortunately, although I was stumbling along and still in a daze, it didn't take long to get to our house. She let go of my hand, opened the door and led me to a large chair in our living room. She said, "Just sit quietly now. I've gotta get back to school but I know you're gonna be OK. Can I get you a glass of water or something before I go?" I still wasn't able to speak but shook my head "no" and tried to smile. Miss Thurman closed the door behind her and I began my exile from Paron School. It was still about a month before school ended but I never did return to school and I never did finish the seventh grade.

After Miss Thurman left, I relaxed and enjoyed the quietness. I continued to wonder what was wrong with me and tried to sing a song that I knew very well but I wasn't able to make a sound. I tried reciting the alphabet and I could do it in my head but couldn't say it. I thought of Jesus and God sitting on their thrones hoping they would help me and then I got mad at them because they hadn't helped me at all. On the other hand, I figured it might be my fault since I hadn't been reading the Bible lately and I hadn't been to church since living in Paron.

I fell asleep again and slept for an hour or so and would have slept even longer but the front door opened and that woke me up. Mom, Dad and Joan walked into the house with a very concerned look on their faces. Miss Thurman had talked to Mom and Dad and told them about my strange behavior. Mom was the first to speak to me, "Can you say your name?"

"Sure," I said in an unsteady voice that seemed strange to me. Then I said slowly with several starts and stops, "It's James Lester Good Jr." After I said my name, I was surprised how hard it was to talk even though I could form the words in my head, but I was a little relieved that I could talk at all. Even so, it took a couple of days being away from school before I could talk in my normal way again.

Dad said, "He's been in shock and it's not surprising considerin what a hell-hole Paron has been for him."

Mom agreed, and said, "You'll be OK and your Dad and I've talked about it and we don't want you to go back to school here. There's only

CONFRONTATIONS

a month left anyway and we don't want you to go through any more of what you've already been through."

And Dad added, "Joan, you've had it bad too and you don't have to go back either."

Joan replied, "If it doesn't get any worse, I'd rather just stick it out. It's been bad but I haven't had it nearly as tough as Junior and I think he'll be a lot better off staying home."

Joan was right; being a girl had been an advantage. She didn't have any friends, she was the object of insults and she was never invited to any social events including her Junior class prom. It was common for smart girls to be harassed and for tall girls to be harassed. Joan received double harassment because she was both tall and smart. But the other students hadn't yelled in her face, hadn't spit on her, punched her, or written a song about wishing she was dead. And I was pleased that Joan stuck up for me.

By staying home, I soon recovered and enjoyed my time away from school very much. I still had all my schoolbooks and read them during the day. I knew how much material my teachers planned to cover in the school year so I made sure I read at least as much as the students that were still in class read. It wasn't hard to keep up because the material wasn't very hard. We still had a radio that we had bought in Portland that could receive a couple of radio stations. As a diversion from my studies, I would listen to a famous Arkansas religious quartet from 12:30 p.m. to 1:00 p.m. called the "Stamp-Baxter Melody Boys" that was aired over radio station KARK in Little Rock. It was ironic that the sponsor of this program was Magic Miller's Best Flour, the very flour Mom used to buy and whose sacks she used to make our clothes from. Then at 2:00 p.m. I would listen to "Pools Paradise" a program of slapstick humor that was famous for the weird sound effects used generously throughout the program. A couple of times some school kids would leave the playground and start to come over to our house with the idea to harass me. I was pleased, though, that my neighbor, Mr. Smetna, kept a look out for these confrontations and would rush out of his house on his wagon yelling at the kids to behave and to get back to school. He could make ferocious facial expressions when he wanted to and he backed up his expressions with a sawed off shotgun that he sometimes kept on his lap. The kids did what he said, and soon they stopped coming altogether.

The school year ended on a Wednesday at noon and about an hour later a truck that Dad had arranged for arrived from Conway to move us. Dad and Mom had planned for sometime to not spend a minute more in Paron than we had to so we were very happy when the truck arrived. The movers had no trouble packing and loading our belongings in less than an hour. While they were loading the truck, I went next door and said good-bye to Mr. Smetna and thanked him for protecting our house and me. He took his gloves off and shook my hand. It was the first time I had seen his bare hands and I considered it an honor that he would take his gloves off to shake hands. He said he didn't like the noise the other kids made so when he ran them off, he was protecting his privacy as well as protecting me. Mr. Smetna had turned out to be a good friend and not nearly as grumpy as he first seemed.

We got inside Suzy as fast as we could and drove down the road away from Paron and headed for our new home in Conway. Although we were overjoyed to leave Paron behind, the traumatic events of the past school year had left us subdued and very quiet during our car ride. Joan was happy that she had survived the harassment, finished the eleventh grade and had only one more year before she would leave home and live an independent life. The harassment from her classmates had left her exhausted, however, and she had come very close to dropping out of school. Mom had been nervous at the beginning of the school year because she had almost no teaching experience and was afraid she would fail. It turned out, though, she was a big hit with her third grade students and they had been too young to join in the harassment that the rest of us experienced. And on her last day of class, many of her students brought her presents to show their appreciation. I was relieved because I had recovered from what I first thought was some type of permanent brain damage but it turned out to be a temporary, though serious, stupor caused by too much stress. I kept thinking about the kindness of Mr. Smetna and especially about the kindness of Miss Thurman. I have always been grateful to her because at the peak of my crisis she rescued me from the other students, held my hand and walked me home. I was also grateful that Dad, Mom and even Joan had been so supportive when I dropped out of the seventh grade. We were a strange family in many respects but when I was faced with a critical emergency, my family was totally loyal and supportive. I was hurt and confused by God and Jesus' behavior. I had accepted them and prayed to them but they didn't help me. I confided to Mom how hurt I was by Jesus ignoring me but she said that wasn't the case and that I should thank Jesus for sending Miss Thurman to me. I asked Mom why Jesus just didn't stop the kids from mistreating me in the first place and she said that He worked in mysterious ways. Well, things did turn out all right I guess but it sure was hurtful and confusing. Dad was the most subdued of us all. He was pleased that he had finished the school year without backing down to the student protestors but he also knew he should have graded their papers and kept records. He had been fired as he thought he would be, but he had a better teaching job already lined up for the next school year.

As if to join us in celebrating our move from Paron, Suzy was on her best behavior. She traveled forty miles before boiling over—a new record for her.

CHAPTER 8

Seeking Verification

THE DIRT ROAD leading out of Paron was now several miles behind us as was the hated Paron school, the unfriendly trees, hostile grocery store clerks and ticks. We were on highway 64 just on the outskirts of Conway, enjoying a smooth ride on fresh pavement and with Suzy on good behavior. Houses on both sides of the highway became more frequent and closer together with an occasional store or gas station built here and there. And soon there were some familiar sights. Entering Conway again was like greeting an old friend after a long absence. I remembered the small apartment we had lived in when we first arrived from Portland. I remembered my trip to Conway in Howie's Chicken Coop when we lived in Republican, and I remembered the sad day when we auctioned off our horse, Bird, and her mule colt, Red. Now Conway would be our home for, "as far as I can see," Dad told us.

"Look, there's our old apartment!" Joan said with unusual excitement in her voice. "Yes," Dad agreed, "We're on Davis Street again and like I told everyone, our new home's just a few blocks away from our old apartment. So, you already know something about the neighborhood."

We drove a few more blocks and then made a sharp right turn and pulled about 10 yards into a driveway. Dad cut Suzy's engine and reached for the door handle. "Wait," Mom said urgently and gently placed her hand on Dad's arm to stop him from opening the door. "I want us to sit here just a while and look at the house before we go in. That's important." And she was right—it did seem important although I couldn't exactly explain why. We were looking at our new home at 517 Davis Street in Conway, Arkansas. We had been hearing about the house ever since Dad told us he had bought it but it was hard to believe that we were finally only a few feet away from it. I could tell that Dad was annoyed by Mom's plea to just sit and look because he had already seen the house several times and was impatient to get inside. But he decided to please Mom and pulled his hand back from the door.

Dad pointed towards the back of the house, "Now that side door over there—I've told you about it before—it'll make it easy for Bill to come and go as he needs to without waking up the rest of us. It opens right into that back bedroom and I think he's gonna like it." Dad and Mom were convinced that Bill would move out of the small room he was renting a few miles away on the other side of Conway and move in with us. Mom started to say something but Joan, who had been squirming in pain for some time but was afraid to say anything, finally spoke up, "I've gotta go to the bathroom! Now!" Mom told Joan not to talk about going to the bathroom in front of men but with a sigh of resignation opened Suzy's door and said with exasperation, "Well, I was hoping we could sit still and look at the house a bit longer but I guess we can't so let's get inside. Joan, you oughta learn to control yourself, young lady!"

Joan ran into the house but the rest of us took our time and walked leisurely across the lawn. We passed by a big tree in the front yard that had branches perfectly grown for me to climb. But most importantly, I could tell it was a friendly tree and a very welcome change from the ominous, unfriendly ones we left behind in Paron. We walked up a couple of steps to the front door that Joan had left open in her rush to get to the bathroom. The living room, just on the other side of the door, was large and filled with boxes of our belongings that had been packed in Paron and unloaded a short time earlier by the movers. Mom said she was really pleased with the size of the living room but didn't understand why there were so many electrical outlets on the wall and why they were so high up. They were a good four feet from the floor she guessed. "You never told me about these sockets," Mom said. Dad explained that when the house was built, the living room had been designed to be a Laundromat and had been used as a Laundromat for a couple of years. The outlets made it easy to plug all the washing machines and dryers into. Now the Conway zoning laws wouldn't allow a Laundromat at this location but Dad explained, "It was different a few years back when the house was built. And the outlets aren't gonna bother anything or anybody. Besides those high-up sockets make it easy to plug things into or out of—you can just stand up and do it! No need to bend over like you gotta do with most sockets! And I was able to bargain some money off the price cause they're so high up. We got a good deal!" After hearing Dad's explanation, Mom gave him one of her specialized looks of disgust and shook her head.

Next to the living room was a large master bedroom where the movers had set up two beds. One was for Dad and Mom and the other one was for me. Although I had shared bedrooms with my siblings, I had only shared a bedroom with my parents on a temporary basis and I didn't like the thought of sharing on a permanent basis. The second bedroom was for Joan and to be shared with Marie if she ever visited us. But that was unlikely—we hadn't seen her since she stormed out of our house in Portland after a brutal fight with J.C. The third bedroom, the one with the private entrance we saw when we looked out from Suzy, was reserved for Bill.

We liked our new house very much and the most likeable thing about it was the running water in the kitchen and bathroom. Our homes in Paron, Liberty and Republican did have electricity but not running water and we longed for it again like we had in Portland and Vancouver. I turned on both kitchen faucets and was overjoyed to see water run out. I splashed my hands in the stream and then splashed some on my face but stopped abruptly—I realized too late that I had splashed some on the floor. But to my surprise, neither Mom nor Dad yelled at me. And Dad came over put his hands in the stream and splashed some on Mom who giggled and seemed pleased by his attention. She splashed him back. It was the first time I had seen my parents being playful like that and it was fun to watch. At about the same time, I heard the toilet flush and Joan opened the bathroom door with a great big grin on her face. She was also delighted at having our very own indoor water supply once again.

One of the main reasons that Dad and Mom bought our Davis Street house was its convenient location to schools, churches—in particular to a Church of Christ—and to a neighborhood grocery store. For some time, they had been studying college courses by correspondence administered by the Arkansas State Teachers College (ASTC) but now we lived only a few blocks away from the actual campus and they planned to continue their studies on site. I had been enrolled in the ASTC Training School that was established to give the ASTC students learning to be teachers practical classroom experience. The Training School offered classes from the first through eighth grades and although I hadn't finished seventh grade, Dad had created all the necessary papers to get me accepted in the eighth grade. I was fortunate to be accepted because the Training School was one of the best in Arkansas supervised by Norm Westin who had a passionate devotion to a solid, liberal-arts oriented curriculum and he demanded and received the best from the student teachers that were assigned to teach our classes. I was to learn that he also demanded the best from the students.

My entry into the school got off to a disastrous start. The first day of school was devoted to orientation and was fairly easy. We were assigned our desks, the teachers were introduced and the curriculum for the coming school year was explained. Then, each of us in turn stood up by our desk, introduced ourselves and gave a little background information. That's when I learned that all the other students had been classmates before—I was the only new one in the group. I was still shattered from my Paron experience and didn't want to talk to anyone let alone stand up and speak in public. Although the other students seemed polite and friendly, I could feel my throat tighten and my stomach beginning to make knots at the thought of speaking publicly. In any case when it came my turn I spoke my name softly, while looking at the floor, and added that I had transferred from the school in Paron. Then I sat down rapidly and was momentarily relieved that my part was over. But Mr. Westin wanted more and said, "And what else, Lester. I know you've got a lot more to tell us than that." I shook my head "no" and hoped I would be left alone. But Mr. Westin didn't leave me alone. It was obvious he had talked to my parents because he was very familiar with my background and said to the class, "Well, it looks like Lester isn't going to tell us more so *I'm* going to tell you more about him." And he told the class that I had lived in Oregon and Washington, had already gone to seven different schools, had survived a major school fire that destroyed the whole school and that during World War II the farm house that I lived in had been taken over by the Army. I was embarrassed to hear all that but the other kids thought that made me exotic and interesting. And unlike the kids in

Paron, having lived in Oregon and Washington was a positive factor, not because they agreed with integration, but because they had studied the states of the union in the seventh grade and thought all the states on the West Coast were especially beautiful and exotic. When our first school day was finished, I left the classroom as fast as possible because I was too shy to socialize.

The disaster began on the second day of class. Right at the beginning of the day, Mr. Westin told us that we were to elect student officers and hold regular class room meetings at least every two weeks and at any other times if needed. The officers to be elected were a president, vice president, secretary and treasurer, and the class meetings were to be planned and run by the president. He told us to first elect our president and that the floor was open for nominations. He added that the student making the nomination was to say a few words as to why their nominee should be elected. All the other students had been in a class with Mr. Westin before and were familiar with the election process but it was new to me. Anyway, Peggy raised her hand and nominated Kent for president. She said Kent would do a good job because he had been the president of the seventh grade and had proved himself doing that job. I thought it was a good nomination too because Kent had an out-going personality and he struck me as a natural leader. Then came a stomach turning shock—to my dismay, another student, Carol, nominated me for president! I shook my head "no" and cried out, "No. I don't want it!" My protests didn't stop Carol from saying that I should be president because I had a background different from everyone else and she thought I would do interesting things that would be exciting. Mr. Westin said that the rule was that I had to accept the nomination unless the person that nominated me withdrew the nomination and that the rest of the class agreed. So he asked to show by voice vote if my nomination should be withdrawn and there was a large chorus of "no" and not a single "yes." Then, Mr. Westin announced that the nominations for president were closed and that Kent and I were to cast our secret ballots for president and leave the room while the rest of the students cast their secret ballots. I voted for Kent and I was pretty sure that Kent voted for himself so that was two votes already for him. I was beginning to feel better because I was getting more confident that Kent would win and I wouldn't have to be president. When we were

BORROWED BIBLES

outside the room, Kent looked at me angrily and said he sure hoped I would lose. And I replied sincerely, "So do I. I don't wanta be president and you just saw that I tried to withdraw." Then, I turned my back to Kent, closed my eyes and prayed anxiously to Jesus to let me lose. I kept praying until Mr. Westin opened the door and told us the election was over and we should come back to class.

"Well, Lester, you are now Mr. President!" Mr. Westin loudly announced as Kent and I walked back inside the room. "Here's your gavel. This'll be your first class meeting to run and in today's meeting I want you to complete the selection of the class officers, the Vice President, the Secretary and the Treasurer." Then, he put his arm around Kent and the two of them walked to their seats, sat down and looked at me expectantly. They weren't the only ones looking at me. The whole class had their eyes focused on me and were waiting for me to lead the class meeting—but I didn't know how to do it. Their looks went from pleasant anticipation, to curiosity, and then to impatience, but I stood mute not knowing what to say or do. It became very quiet in the room and some of the students started fidgeting but I couldn't figure out what to do. I began to feel like I had felt in Paron when I became so stressed that I hid in a closet and lost my voice. Yet, while the stress was of similar degree it was of a different kind. At Paron the students had greeted me with hatred but during this class meeting I was greeted with impatience and disappointment. Still, I didn't say or do anything and I was frozen in my thoughts. Kent started to grin at my failure to lead the class. Even with all the pressure, however, I didn't know what to do so I finally just admitted it and said out loud what everyone had figured out, "I don't know what to do." Some of the students were embarrassed for me but others laughed and Kent's grin turned into a sneer. Mr. Westin came to my rescue. "OK, come sit down. We all have to learn sometime so I'm going to run the rest of the class meeting this time and finish electing the other officers. Lester, I want you to watch carefully because in two weeks the next class meeting will be yours to run. And don't count on me to help you." I slinked back to my seat and watched and concentrated as hard as I could on what Mr. Westin was doing. After class, I could tell that my classmate's opinion of me had gone from curiosity and respect to disdain and puzzlement.

The next class meeting while not as bad as the first was still a failure. I didn't have a thought-out agenda, I didn't control the questions, I didn't interact with the Secretary or Treasurer, and I didn't close the meeting properly. The next meeting was also awful and the next and the next and so on. After each meeting, Mr. Westin or some other teacher would review my performance with me and make suggestions but I kept making very embarrassing mistakes because of my ignorance and lack of confidence. And several of the students let me know how letdown they felt because of my poor performance. It was especially hurtful when Carol, the girl that had nominated me, told me that she had initially thought I was an experienced city boy but I had turned out to be just a backward country boy and she wished she hadn't nominated me. A few days before a class meeting, my stress level would rise drastically and more than once I felt like quitting the Training school and staying home but I knew my parents wouldn't let me do that. There were a few times I told Mom I was too sick to go to school and while she was sympathetic to real illnesses, she was able to see when I was saying I was sick just to get out of running the class meeting and she made me go to school anyway. As it was, I didn't miss a single day of class but it wasn't until the end of the school year that I finally learned to carry out the duties of the president in a way that Mr. Westin said was OK. His words were accurate: it had taken me several months to do just an "OK" job—it would have taken many more months to do a "good" job.

My role as class president was stressful, but the subjects we studied in class were very interesting and stimulating—especially the subjects of music, poetry and art. We were exposed to classical music appreciation and I loved it and looked forward to hearing each recording the teacher selected to play and discuss. I especially remember the days we heard *Peter and the Wolf*, *Swan Lake*, *Grand Canyon Suite* and shorter pieces such as the *Saber Dance* and *Flight of the Bumble Bee*. Of course, these were some of the easier classical music pieces to listen to and learn about but this introductory step was important because up to then I knew virtually nothing about classical music or music in general. What music I had been exposed to was in the Religious or Country genre with an occasional Western selection. And for the first time I discovered poetry that I understood and loved—Robert Frost wrote it. His poetry had

BORROWED BIBLES

a remarkably positive effect on me. I felt like I had met a friend who was moved by nature as I was moved but he was able to express his feelings while I was not. He was an inspiration to me and he would be joined later by other great men that inspired me including Mozart, Einstein and Euler. We were also exposed to the art and life of famous artists such as Paul Gauguin, Pablo Picasso and the Mexican artist, Diego Rivera. And while studying Rivera's works, we learned about the history and culture of Mexico and the interaction of the three primary ethnic groups: the Mestizos, Crillos and Indios. We also learned about the religion of the ancient Aztecs and this was especially interesting because it was the only other religion I had studied. But it was a religion that was very strange and awful. They believed in about 1,000 different gods although their sun god was the most important one. And they made human sacrifices to it to insure that the sun would rise and the crops would grow. Equally strange, they believed in 13 heavens and nine underground levels that were similar to but not exactly the same as hell. For some reason Mr. Westin asked me what I thought about the Aztec religion the next time I met with him to review my performance as class president. I answered:

"It's strange and awful. How could so many people believe that stuff?"
"Well, how do we know it's not true?"
"It can't be true cause everyone knows there's just one God."
"But how do we know that?"
"The Bible says so!"
"And how do we know the Bible is true?"
"Because the Bible's the word of God!"
"And how do we know it's the word of God?"

Mr. Westin asked all his questions in a calm, sincere way but he could see that I was getting exasperated by them and said:
"Look, I know you want to be a preacher and I know you'll be a better preacher if you figure out how you know what you're preaching is really true. I'm not just talking about religion—ask yourself how you know that the newspaper you read is true. How do you know what I say or your teachers say is true? Think about this real hard! Now,

SEEKING VERIFICATION

enough—let's talk about that last class meeting you ran and how you could've done it better."

So I listened to him tell me how to be a better class president but it was hard to pay attention. First, I had learned about the awful Aztec religion—then, I was surprised and confused how the supervisor of our school could be asking how I knew their religion wasn't true when the answer was obvious.

At the same time we were studying liberal arts courses, we were also studying current events in interesting and creative ways. For example, the year I attended in 1948 happened to be a presidential election year and we learned about the general election process and nomination process as well as the role the Electoral College played. We brought newspaper articles to class about the latest happenings on the campaign trail and discussed them. In addition, Mr. Westin announced that we would have our own presidential election to coincide with the actual one. So as a learning process, he and the faculty selected three students—one to run as a representative for Harry Truman of the Democratic Party, one as a representative for Thomas Dewey of the Republican Party and one as a representative for Strom Thurmond of the new State's Rights Party better known as the Dixiecrat Party. I was not doing a good job as class president so I was surprised to be selected to represent Truman and tried to get out of doing it but Mr. Westin wouldn't let me. We were given two weeks to campaign during the lunch hour in any reasonable way we saw fit, including placing campaign banners around the school property. At the end of the two-week campaign period, we were to give one speech to the class lasting no more than 15 minutes. Then the class was to vote for President of the United States. I was really at a loss about campaigning but I put up a few banners with one of Truman's slogans on it, "Pour it on 'em, Harry." I thought about using Truman's more famous slogan, "Give 'em hell, Harry," but it didn't seem right to use the word "hell" since we didn't use that word in our family unless we were very careful about it; we usually said "the place below." But I thought I did have one advantage because the parents of most of the students were Democrats and I thought this would help influence them to vote for me. On the other hand, there was a lot of enthusiasm for the Dixiecrat, Strom Thurmond, and my classmate, Kent, who represented him. Kent had been my opponent as class president and

BORROWED BIBLES

now he was my opponent for the U.S. President and I was impressed with the good job he did campaigning. Kent put up lots of banners with the Dixiecrat's "Segregation Forever!" slogan on it—a slogan all the students agreed with except me. I hadn't made up my mind yet because I had enjoyed going to the integrated schools in Washington and Oregon but I was also concerned that maybe God wanted segregation as many in Arkansas believed. Larry, who represented the Republican, Tom Dewey, was also a good campaigner but there was very little support for Republicans in Arkansas so I figured Larry didn't have a chance to win and that the contest would be between Kent and me. On the big day of our speeches, Kent, Larry and I did our best to persuade the students to vote for us but I believed that they all had their minds already made up and our speeches wouldn't have much effect. Kent gave an entertaining and persuasive speech and had the students applauding, laughing and shaking their heads in agreement several times. He also pointed out that President Truman had recently signed an order integrating the armed services and that alone was a good reason to not vote for Harry Truman. Larry and I were dull by comparison. My speech, while factual in nature summarizing the impressive accomplishments of Truman, didn't contain any inspirational slogans to capture the students' attention. I was the last one to speak and when I finished, Mr. Westin told the three of us to cast our vote by secret ballot and then to leave the room while the other students voted by secret ballot. While we were waiting outside our classroom, Kent told Larry and me that he was sure he had won because he had run a better campaign and given a much better speech. Frankly, I thought he was right.

Mr. Westin opened the door to the classroom and told us to come back in because the votes had been counted. After we walked in and before we returned to our seats, Mr. Westin held out his hand to me and said, "Congratulations, Mr. Truman, you've won and are the next President of the United States!" The rest of the students applauded. Now I was not only class president but also a make-believe President of the United States but that didn't bother me too much because the election was over and there wouldn't be any additional duties to cause additional stress. Later at lunchtime, it was Kent whom the other students crowded around and congratulated on a great campaign. I had received the most votes because of the support that the real Harry

SEEKING VERIFICATION

Truman had but Kent was the emotional winner of our election. Larry did even worse than I thought he would and received just one vote, presumably his own.

(The actual 1948 presidential election produced the greatest upset in the history of the United States. Virtually every poll incorrectly predicted that the Republican, Thomas Dewey, would be the winner. The final vote tally showed, however, that while Dewey did win 16 states, Truman won 28 including Arkansas, and Thurmond won 4. There was also another significant candidate, Henry Wallace of the Progressive Party, who won almost as much of the popular vote as Thurmond but didn't win a single state.)

My Family, November 1948, 517 Davis Street, Conway, Arkansas
Sister Joan, Brother J.C., Brother Bill, Mom, Dad, Me
J.C. was visiting from Florida. Sister Marie, not present, lived in Alaska

It was a comfortable 15-minute walk from our house to the Conway Church of Christ. I started attending their Sunday school the first Sunday we lived on Davis Street and after Sunday school was over, I impatiently waited for the adult church service to begin and I would attend that too. For a while, Dad, Mom and Joan who left the house later than I did would join me in the church service and we would sit together. But after about a month, Joan stopped attending and Mom and Dad allowed it because she was a senior in high school and only a few months away from leaving home. And Mom and Dad stopped coming to church because they needed the time to do their college homework. It had been a long time since Dad had held church services at home. His beliefs shaped by his Church of Christ background were as strong as ever but when he became more occupied with college work, he stopped being active in the church. In contrast, I enjoyed going to church so much that I sometimes attended the adult services held on Wednesday evening in addition to Sunday school and Sunday church services. Mom worried about me coming home late in the evening and she also worried about the amount of time I was spending on church matters. She didn't think it was healthy for someone at my age of 12 to spend so much time with adult church services and told me, "I never thought I'd wind up worrying about a child of mine going to church too much!" At the same time she was relieved that I wasn't getting into trouble like some boys in the neighborhood so she didn't make me reduce my church time.

Between my church attendance and Training School activities, I was very busy but I was learning a lot and quite happy. My biggest problem continued to be the stress caused by being the class president. But attending church services and watching our preacher, Jack Reed, deliver a sermon helped me to speak better when I conducted a class meeting and helped me in later years when I spoke in public. I soon learned by watching him that it was not only his words that caught the congregation's attention but also his well-timed gestures such as chopping the air with his hands, pointing his finger and clinching his fist for emphasis, changing the loudness of his voice—first a shout, then a whisper—pacing back and forth and speaking from different positions. He amplified his gestures with his facial expressions that he could change instantly and he knew exactly how to use the baptistery—painted with a mural of a lake and large trees—as a theatrical backdrop. A few times he really got dramatic, jumped up and down, took off his tie and threw it on the floor. I didn't plan on ever doing that.

Preacher Reed's sermons were often based on the parables of Jesus and how they could be used to help us lead a good life and enter heaven someday. I had read the parables before but Preacher Reed went into detailed explanations and provided a lot of examples about what could be learned from them. That sometimes caused a problem since he gave so many examples that his sermons seemed endless and I often lost interest. I learned to tell when he was, thankfully, coming to the end of his sermon because he would always find a way to remind us that in order to get to heaven, belief in Jesus was necessary but it wasn't enough—we had to be baptized by total immersion in water and he was ready to do it. He would point to the baptistery and remind us that it was waiting for us so what were we waiting for? "Come to Jesus!" he would say while chopping the air with his clenched fist.

Even though his sermons were usually too long, I looked forward to them because he was such a good speaker and knew a lot about the Bible. And for years I had been saving questions about the Bible for the day when I could talk to a Church of Christ preacher about them. I had hoped that some of my questions would be answered in his sermons without me specifically asking but if they weren't, then I planned to make an appointment with him to get them answered. Then, one Sunday, his sermon was about one of the most important and long-standing questions I had, "Did God want segregation or integration?" Preacher Reed was clear and adamant, "God wanted segregation!" And he addressed this subject in his sermon because President Truman had just a few months earlier, in July 1948, issued Executive Order 9981 that ordered integration of the armed services to provide, "equality of treatment and opportunity for all persons in the armed services without regard to race, color, religion or national origin." Preacher Reed said this was a sinful step in and of itself but he was worried that this would just be the beginning of a lot of steps that would eventually lead to full-scale integration like "the Yankee states had." Or as he put it, Truman's sinful order was like the camel that first stuck his nose in the tent but wouldn't be satisfied with just that—no, the camel would only be satisfied by taking over the whole tent. Preacher Reed explained that God had commanded that there be segregation and it was documented in the Bible. God commanded it at the beginning, in Genesis, when He told all the living things to reproduce "After his own kind." And "own kind" definitely meant the same color. Further, God believed so strongly in segregation that in Deuteronomy, He gave detailed examples of things that shouldn't be mixed—for example, an ass and an ox shouldn't plow together, and garments of "diverse sorts" such as wool and linen shouldn't be worn together. And the clinching argument was that in heaven there would be segregation as proven in Revelation where the 12 tribes of Israel, numbering 12,000 people each, would be kept as separate entities. I had read Revelation several times and frankly it never did make sense to me so I was glad that Preacher Reed explained that part of it. I had also read the passages in Genesis and Deuteronomy and found that information much easier to understand. When he finished with his sermon and his explanations, I could understand why so many people believed that God wanted segregation. But at the same time the passages were mysterious enough that I could also understand why the preachers I had known about in Washington and Oregon didn't believe that God wanted segregation. Then, for a moment, I also thought about what Mr. Westin had said when we had discussed the Aztec religion—he asked how I knew the Bible was true. That was a bothersome question, but I decided to postpone thinking about it. For the moment, I was satisfied enough with Preacher Reed's answers that I made a appointment with him to answer my other questions. Then, after he answered them, I would ask to be baptized at the next church service.

On the Sunday morning of my appointment with Preacher Reed I was about as excited as I was on Christmas mornings. I had made sure the day before that all my questions about God, Jesus and the Bible that I had accumulated over the years were written neatly in my notebook and arranged in order of importance. Preacher Reed had told me to be sure to attend his church service as I usually did and to stay till it was over, and he said good-bye to everyone and closed the front door. Then he and I would go to his private office at the back of the church and I could ask my questions.

Mom understood why the day was so important to me and why I was so excited. As a special treat, she offered to fix me anything I wanted for breakfast but I didn't feel like eating. She understood that too and didn't force me to eat so I used the time to review my questions again. She also thought I'd be very happy when I got back from church in the afternoon and promised to make a special supper to celebrate. Dad wasn't home. He had taken a teaching job in Damascus, a small

SEEKING VERIFICATION

town about 20 miles north of Conway, and he often stayed there over the weekend. I had hoped he would be home to wish me luck and I was sure he'd be proud that I had arranged a private meeting with Preacher Reed. Joan also realized how important the day was for me and even took the time to say good-bye.

The walk to church seemed longer than usual and so did Sunday school. I had thought of skipping Sunday school and only showing up for the church service to listen to the Preacher's sermon. That way I would have an extra hour or so to review my questions and better prepare myself for my meeting with him. As it was, I wasted time because instead of paying attention to the Sunday school lesson, I kept reviewing the questions over and over in my head. It was while I was doing this that I realized that the questions I had didn't matter very much if the Bible weren't true—a possibility I would never have even considered if Mr. Westin hadn't recently asked me how I knew it was true.

After Sunday school was over, I walked to the church auditorium, chose a bench close to the church's front door and sat next to the aisle that ran through the middle of church. I was several minutes early on purpose to make sure I would get a good view of the baptistery at the other end of the church and the door next to it. Soon, Preacher Reed came through the door, said an opening prayer, made some announcements and joined the church choir in a hymn. Then, he turned to delivering a sermon based on the famous story in the Book of John of a woman who was caught in the act of adultery. Some Pharisees brought her before Jesus and Jesus was asked if she should be stoned as dictated by the Law of Moses. (When Preacher Reed said the word "stoned," he emphasized the word by hurling an imaginary stone into the audience.) This put Jesus in a complicated position because if he said she shouldn't be stoned, then he was in violation of the Law. On the other hand, Jesus had been preaching the forgiveness of sins so if he agreed with the stoning, then he contradicted himself. But Jesus didn't choose either of these paths. Instead, he spoke the famous words, "He that is without sin among you, let him first cast a stone at her." The Pharisees apparently hadn't expected this response, were confused and responded by walking away and leaving Jesus alone with the woman. Jesus uttered more famous words, "Neither do I condemn thee: go, and sin no more." I had always liked this story very much for it shows that Jesus was compassionate and could break with a Law that was cruel. There was something, however, about the dramatic way that Preacher Reed described how the Pharisees walked away and left Jesus and the woman alone (Preacher Reed shouted "a-LONE!") that prompted a question I had never thought of before. If they were alone, how do we know what was said? Well, I certainly hadn't expected to think of another question just before I was to meet with Preacher Reed but it was an important question.

After the sermon was finished, the collection plate was passed, there was a closing prayer and the congregation was dismissed. Preacher Reed stood by the front door and said good-bye to each of the people attending worship. I stood aside at a respectful distance waiting for my appointment. When he said the last good-bye, he closed the door, gave me a warm smile and said, "Now, Lester, let's go have that talk." And he put his arm gently around me and we walked down the aisle to his private office.

Preacher Reed sat behind his desk, and although there was a small fan running and blowing air on him, he was sweating anyway and wiped his brow with a handkerchief. Then he asked, "OK, what're your questions?" I had rehearsed what I was going to say many times but I was still nervous. I took a deep breath, opened my notebook and responded, "I've got lots of questions but first I'd like you to tell me how we know the Bible is true." Preacher Reed didn't say anything for a long time. His office had been very quiet anyway but he turned off the fan to make it even quieter and he continued to glare at me with a mixture of disbelief and anger. His eyes narrowed to slits and he pointed a finger at me and said:

"How could you even think that question let alone ask it? You've been coming to Sunday school, church and Wednesday evening meetings and you've read the Bible a lot and you wanta be a preacher. Then, you surely should know you don't do something like doubt the Bible. Because if you doubt the Bible you doubt God and you doubt Jesus and you know what that means, right?"

But it really wasn't a question. I could tell he didn't expect an answer and he continued:

"It means, what it says in John 3:18 that if you don't believe, you're already condemned. Don't you understand? You're condemned! Why? Because the devil is surely inside you that's why and I wouldn't be surprised if he found you over at that fancy Training School you go to. But it's not too late. Now, you come with me."

And with his hand firmly on my shoulder, he led me out of his office. We walked to the front of the baptistery and faced it; he got down on his knees and told me to do the same. I got on my knees next to him and he prayed:

"God, this boy has the devil in him and has doubts about your word and your Bible. Forgive him, God. He is a sinner but he's young and the devil took advantage of him. Help him close the door to all his doubts. Help him open that wonderful door that leads to faith in you, faith in Jesus and faith in the Holy Ghost. Amen!"

He continued to pray quietly and I could tell from his clenched eyes that he was praying with passion. Then, he said:

"Now, I want you to go home and keep on praying. Then, next Sunday I want you to walk up that aisle, accept Jesus and get baptized. You're old enough to be baptized now. And as you pray, remember that you're condemned but Jesus will forgive you—but you've got to have faith. You've got to stop questioning the Bible because when you question the Bible you question God and Jesus."

With that, he walked me up the aisle to the front door of the church, opened it and said a curt good-bye with anger still in his voice.

On my walk back home I stumbled a few times much as I had stumbled the day I abandoned my classes at Paron School. I wondered if I had also lost my voice again so I tried reciting the alphabet out loud and found that I could so that made me feel better. But I was hurt and disappointed and most of all I felt betrayed by Preacher Reed. For years I had been preparing for a meeting like the one I just had with him only to find out that by asking questions I would be condemned. As I walked and stumbled along, I passed other kids about my age that were riding bicycles and playing in the street. I envied them and felt foolish for having a notebook under my arm with questions about religion that I never got to ask. I felt like I had wasted my time and I wished I had spent more time riding a bicycle and playing like other 12-year-old kids. I also dreaded what Mom was going to say when she found out why Preacher Reed got so mad at me. I was even more afraid of what Dad would do when he found out later.

I didn't return to the Conway Church of Christ, I didn't get baptized and I gave up my plan to be a preacher. My thoughts and feelings were jumbled and I wasn't sure what I believed about religion, but I was as sure as I could be that it was wrong to be condemned for asking questions about it. Mom's reaction was that I shouldn't question the Bible but accept it on faith, but she also said asking questions wasn't a sin and Preacher Reed shouldn't have told me it was. I was relieved when I found out later that Dad agreed with her. I was afraid, though, that Preacher Reed would come to our house and talk to my parents directly about my questioning and for not being baptized like he had directed. I wasn't sure what my parents would do then. It turned out, however, that it didn't matter very much because I learned that we would be leaving Conway soon and moving to the small town of Tinsman, Arkansas where I would be in the ninth grade and Dad and Mom would be schoolteachers. I had just graduated from the Training School's eighth grade, and Joan had graduated from Conway High School. She moved with us to Tinsman but didn't stay with us for long. She was eager to move out and be independent and our brother J.C. gave her that opportunity. He asked her to move to Florida and live with him and his wife, Corky—Joan was paid to take care of Pamela Jayne, the newborn first child of J.C. and Corky. We sold our Davis Street house and Dad worked out an agreement with the new owners for Bill, who had moved into the third bedroom as hoped, to continue living there while he attended Arkansas State Teachers College.

* * * * * *

One advantage of our lifestyle of moving every year was that the move would bring an end to some problems. I was glad to leave Conway and get far away from Preacher Reed and his church but I would miss the Training School, Mr. Westin and some of my classmates that had become good friends. And before I moved from Conway I went to visit Mr. Westin. The Training School was closed for the summer but, as I thought, Mr. Westin was in his office tending to administrative duties. I thanked him for all the help he had given me in making me a better class president. But I also wanted him to know that the encouragement he gave me to ask questions got me into a lot of trouble with Preacher Reed. As a matter of fact, I told him, I was condemned according to the preacher who quoted John 3:18 as proof. Mr. Westin said he was sorry for the trouble but that happened sometimes with questions. He added that he had read the Bible a lot too and there was another verse in John I should remember and that was John 8:32, "And ye shall know the truth, and the truth shall make you free."

"But," Mr. Westin added as he walked me to the door, "finding out what is true can be hard work. Maybe what I've told you isn't true but maybe what Preacher Reed said to you isn't true either. Maybe we're both wrong. It's up to you to figure it out. Think about it and good luck with the rest of your life."

PART II

CHAPTER 9

Revelations

IT WAS 1970 and I was 34 years old. Twenty two years had passed since I had two life-changing events in 1948: the devastating reprimand by Preacher Reed for questioning the Bible and, in sharp contrast, the positive encouragement from Mr. Westin to question the truth of everything. I went through a period of disorientation and contemplation that ultimately led me to form intertwined, fundamental questions that I continually thought about: How could I verify that a god(s) exists? If god exists, what are the implications for me? What is the purpose of my life? Pondering these fundamental questions formed a backdrop as I went about my daily tasks and pursued the usual milestones of life, made more difficult because of our frequent moves of at least once a year. I lived at 31 different addresses by the time I was 20 and attended 13 different schools from the first through the twelfth grades. I graduated from Glenwood Arkansas High School in 1952, from Washington State University with a degree in electrical engineering in 1956, and married Laura Lawrence in 1959. Our daughter, Marian, was born in 1961 and our son, James Lester III, in 1963. I had held jobs of Design Engineer, Manager of Product Research, Manager of Engineering, Manager of Military Sales and Product Manager. But no matter what my occupation was or whatever milestone I was trying to meet, I continuously pondered the fundamental questions about god and the purpose of life. And in 1970 I pondered extra-hard because there was urgency created by a medical condition that I thought would lead to my death. Plus, coincidentally, Dad had been operated on because he had developed advanced prostate cancer. His recovery wasn't going well and I believed his death was imminent.

Over the years, I had talked with many people and explored numerous books and magazines to learn how others had answered the fundamental questions about god and the purpose of life. It was enlightening when I learned about other religions—especially the Eastern religions of Hinduism and Buddhism. Here were religions older than Christianity and followed by millions of people with concepts of god far different from mine. And in the case of Buddhism there was nothing taught about the creation of the universe or life but instead the teachings were dedicated to increasing the quality of life by reducing sorrow. Buddha was more of a teacher than a prophet and Buddhism more psychotherapy than metaphysics. And it became clear to me that a child born into the world of an Eastern religion would, at least initially, accept the Eastern religious teachings as if there were no choice. This would apply to those born into Judaism or Islam or into any other religion as well—just as I had been presented with Protestant Christianity and accepted it as if there were no choice. And this was an understandable result because my parents were Christians and all the communities I had lived in were Christian. Did this make Christianity right? Wouldn't a member of any other religion be influenced in a similar manner? Was there some test to be made, some experiment to be conducted or some knowledge to be found that could prove that any particular religion was wrong or right? Or was it a matter of faith, of belief and not knowledge?

It was also enlightening to learn that some of the great religious miracles, or myths depending on one's viewpoint, had been repeated throughout history. I found that the great flood story has been told many times as a means that a god had used to cleanse the earth of humans and therefore sin. The epic of Gilgamesh, a Sumerian legend written about 2,000 BCE, is the oldest and describes how a man named Utnapishtim was directed to build a large ark, encompassing an area of one acre, and seven decks high. He loaded the ark with his family and the craftsmen that helped build the ark and the "seed" of all living creatures. Then, there was an immense flood that destroyed all living creatures not in the ark. Water covered everything on the earth except for the top of a mountain where the ark landed. Two birds were sent out at different times but returned because they couldn't find a place to land. Later, a third bird, a raven, was sent and didn't return; therefore, Utnapishtim concluded that the floodwaters had receded. So he and the others emerged from the ark and made a sacrifice to the gods. The legend of Gilgamesh is almost a perfect template for the Noah story. Why do those that accept the Bible as literal truth accept the Noah story but not the other flood legends? Is it a matter of knowledge or a matter of faith and belief? And the flood legends have an unscientific basis to them—there was not nearly enough water in the entire hydrosphere to cover the earth in the ways described. In the Noah legend, for example, more than six hundred million cubic miles of additional water would be needed to do that. Yet, a god could intercede and solve the problem by creating water. If a god could create a universe ex nihilo, then wouldn't that god be able to create as much water as needed? Did a god do that?

It was also surprising to learn how often virgin births were recorded in history. The ancient Egyptians believed in a sun god, Horus, who was born about 3,000 BC to the virgin Isis on December 25. His birth was attended by three wise men; he had 12 disciples, he performed miracles and was crucified, buried in a tomb for three days and resurrected. Mithra was a Persian god fathered by the god, Ahura-Mazda, and born on December 25. He had 12 disciples and shared a last supper with them. He was buried for three days and resurrected. In addition to Horus and Mithra, there were others fathered by a god including Dionysus of Greece and Krishna of India. Many people who live in the West believe these were only myths and not gods but at the same time believe that Jesus was born of a virgin and fathered by god. On the other hand, a god could intercede and cause any of these births to happen. Did a god do that?

Ultimately, I rejected all religious miracles, not just the ones pertaining to great floods and virgin births. They could not have happened unless a god interceded and I concluded that the probability of that happening was close to zero—but I also thought it wrong to conclude that the probability was precisely zero. There is a Mystery beyond human understanding and a fundamental limitation of our knowledge in the sense that we don't know what we don't know. But why couldn't there be a religion that looked to science and reason for guidance rather than to miraculous events? Why couldn't there be a religion that concerns itself with defining what comprises a moral society and then help build it? And I found that there was such a religion. I discovered that the Unitarian church did in fact do that—they looked to deeds not creeds, to reason and not ancient legends. Composed of freethinkers, the church denied the existence of heaven and hell as well as the divinity of Jesus—but agreed that he was a good man. The Unitarians believed that the consequences of one's actions would be felt in this lifetime and not after this life was over. I learned to respect the Unitarians when I read about their beliefs and I respected them even more when I met Laura, my wife-to-be, who had been a lifelong member, as had her family. It was amazing and encouraging to meet this family and other members of the Unitarian church who had unparalleled morals—not because of the threat of hell or the promise of heaven but because it was inherently the good thing to do. I joined the Unitarian church in 1960.

I removed miracles and the gods that created them from my belief system and that was a major and positive step that served as the foundation to my revised religious beliefs; however, that left questions as to what, if anything, I did believe about god. When I first decided to give up being a preacher, I was so disillusioned I didn't think there was anything to believe about god because I concluded there wasn't a god and I became an atheist. It didn't seem possible to me that a god would allow the suffering that living creatures have endured: the black plague, the crusades, the massive flu pandemic of 1918, and the holocaust to name just a few horrible events. And suffering has not been limited to humans. There are millions of animals that are developed enough to feel exquisite pain but are not developed enough to create remedies for these pains. Unless humans intervene, countless animals suffer from wounds or other infections that cause needless pain before there is a merciful death. What kind of god would allow organisms with those limitations to come into being? But I didn't stay an atheist for long. I also thought about the exquisite beauty in the world that brings boundless happiness and wonderful humans that devote their life, and sometimes sacrifice their life, to causes that are uplifting and inspiring. And I also wondered—could something as complex as the universe come into being without a designer and creator? Did god, for some unfathomable reason, bring both happiness and suffering into the world? I finally concluded that I couldn't solve the problem regarding knowledge of god because there wasn't information that could be verified. I concluded that no one else could solve the problem either. When two scientists disagree, there is the potential of proving one (or both) wrong through experiments but when two people have different religious beliefs, there is no experiment that can prove one or both wrong. When I came to this conclusion, I felt elated. By realizing that I couldn't solve the problem, I had, in one respect, actually solved it to my satisfaction. My solution seemed honest and right—a huge load had been lifted off my psyche. And for my benefit as well as for others, I sometimes restated the question about god as a type of algebraic problem. That is, "There are X number of gods but not enough information to solve for X. Further, there is not enough information to prefer one value of X over another." While the problem can't be *solved* through knowledge, it can be (and is) *satisfied* through faith. Indeed, different individuals have assigned many values to X over the years. Atheists believe that X is equal to zero while monotheists believe that X is equal to one. The ancient Aztecs, as I had learned when in the eighth grade, believed that X was about 1,000. To me, X remained an unknown, it is part of the Mystery and I became at peace with the Mystery. I concluded that I didn't have enough faith to be either a theist or an atheist so I stopped being a theist but did not become an atheist. I had become an agnostic. This transition took a long time but was very satisfying to me although it upset my parents and others.

In addition to being an agnostic concerning the existence of god, I also formed an agnostic conclusion about the purpose of life. If there is a "god-given" purpose it cannot be discovered or verified by objective analysis—it is part of the Mystery. I concluded, then, that if I were to have a purpose, I would have to create it myself. And before the year 1970 ended, I accomplished that.

* * * * * *

I had recently visited Dad and Mom in Yakima, Washington where they had retired several years earlier. Mom had warned me before my visit that Dad was very weak and that I'd probably be shocked when I saw him. When she met me at their door, she whispered the same warning to me again. He was sitting in his large, stuffed living room chair that he had used for so many years and although he had a welcoming smile, he didn't attempt to get up and greet me. All his life he had avoided going to doctors except for emergencies and he had never had a regular prostate exam; he thought that exam was especially undignified and unnecessary. And when the pain came, he ignored it as long as he could but it finally overcame him. He then agreed to go to the doctor believing that his problem was a minor one and some type of medication was all that he needed. He was wrong. When prostate cancer spreads to the point that it is painful, it means the cancer is advanced and has spread to other parts of the body. Then, there is no cure but only a possibility of containment. After his prostate was removed, he was prescribed estrogen to slow down the cancer's spread and it was somewhat effective. Unfortunately, Dad discovered that estrogen is a female hormone and after that he didn't have anything to do with it, "That's woman's stuff and I'll die before I take it," he had said defiantly. So, his rampaging untreated cancer combined with the trauma of his recent operation made him very gaunt and weak. He understood that his death was a forgone conclusion and he made the most of his time by watching TV, reading his Bible and singing softly to himself from one of his hymnbooks. The last afternoon of my visit, I pulled up two chairs close to him and asked Mom to sit in one while I sat in the other. This time it was I that passed out the hymnbooks and I noticed that they were the same ones that Dad took from a church over 30 years ago. For my own use, I selected the one that he had written my name in and asked him if he would lead us in *The Old Rugged Cross*. He did, and when we finished singing it, his face was beaming and he wanted to sing some more. So we sang several more hymns stopping in between to catch our breaths and to talk about what we would sing next. I thought after being warmed up from singing hymns, he might get his Bible and read to us from it but he didn't mention it. He did ask if I would go to the store and buy some chili and ice cream for dinner and I gladly did that. That evening Mom served ham and eggs as a main course and for dessert we ate chili and ice cream, a custom we started about thirty years ago for special occasions. There was a lot of talking too; at least between Mom and Dad—I mostly listened as they reminisced about me and my brothers and sisters, their grandchildren and the old days in Arkansas. We avoided talking about religion but I knew both Mom and Dad were curious about what I really believed and about the Unitarian church I belonged to. But they also knew it would be painful for them to hear what I had to say. Dad had told me that since I had chosen to live in California, he wouldn't be surprised if I didn't become somewhat of a hippie and he knew that hippies had very strange religious beliefs. He had been disappointed when I dropped my plans years ago to be a preacher and he had told me so. But when we talked about religion later and he discovered that I was no longer a Christian, he didn't know what to say. It was beyond his comprehension how I could be other than a Christian, yet enjoyed exchanging Christmas presents and occasionally enjoyed singing hymns. Mom also thought I had strange religious beliefs but she wasn't bothered by them. Yet, despite their firm belief in Christianity they had stopped attending church years ago. Dad had strong opinions about how and what preachers should preach and sooner or later every preacher disappointed him. Dad also had an intense dislike for any social interaction with the rest of the congregation so he preferred to stay home. And Mom didn't want to go to church without Dad and so she didn't.

My visit home was cut short by a telephone call from my California office telling me about an emergency in New Jersey centered on electronic equipment our company had lent to their state automotive testing program. It was decided that I should travel to New Jersey and put the problem to rest so I left early to catch a plane back to my office and home in California to prepare for the trip. Dad had slept in his living room chair as he had for many years and he was still in the process of waking up when I said good-bye to him. He told me he was glad for my visit and glad that I sang with him. He said I did pretty good singing out of the hymnbook and he chuckled and said maybe I would turn out to be a preacher after all. He then asked if I would like to take a Bible and a hymnbook with me—specifically, the hymnbook with my name in it. "I've kept it long enough," he said. I told him I would like him to still keep it so that I could sing along with him the next time I visited. He seemed to like that answer, shook my hand and told me to have a safe trip and to take care of his grandchildren. Mom walked me to my rental car that I parked in the driveway and gave me an extra long hug. She always cried when I left from a visit and this was no exception. This time, though, in addition to tears for me leaving, she had tears for Dad and lamented, "I never could get that father of yours to see a doctor!" She held on to my hand and didn't let go until she heard me promise to get doctor exams on a regular basis. It was an easy promise to make because I was frequently in a doctor's office to treat cluster headaches and discuss bothersome chest pains. Satisfied with my promise, she told me to have a safe trip and to take good care of her grandchildren.

* * * * * *

I had been having recurring chest pains for several months and they were getting worse. But I'd convinced myself they weren't serious— merely an inevitable and annoying aspect of my job. I was a member of an engineering team located in the San Francisco Bay Area that was developing an innovative vehicle exhaust pollution analyzer. Finalizing the design required thousands of tests on a variety of cars and trucks and required me to place a probe in their exhaust pipes and take measurements. Doing this for several hours a day, for several months exposed me to enormous amounts of carbon monoxide and hydrocarbons that caused watery eyes, coughs and chest pains. I was sure the chest pains were temporary since I could get rid of them by taking a half-hour break from measuring the exhaust and breathing pure oxygen from a special tank. It always worked and then I would resume the exhaust measurements. But there came a day when oxygen therapy didn't help anymore. Our company had been invited to demonstrate our analyzer in the New Jersey vehicle inspection program and we had accepted because of the experience and good publicity we would get from the demonstration. Initially, our demonstration went well but after a few days of operating, a mysterious problem developed with our analyzer that was too serious to diagnose on the phone. As product manager, I was called to go to New Jersey to solve the problem and to make sure that by the end of the demonstrations the New Jersey personnel were impressed with our analyzer. I was driving up the Bayshore Freeway on the way to the San Francisco airport to catch a plane to New Jersey when chest pain hit so hard that driving became a challenge. I had heard about people having heart attacks and describing their pain like "being hit by a sledge hammer." I thought they were exaggerating—but after experiencing my pain, I agreed with that description. Luckily, I was very close to a freeway exit and to Dr. Owens whom I had been seeing regularly for several years and who was aware of my strange EKG pattern. In the few minutes it took to arrive at his office at the San Mateo Medical Clinic, I was relieved that my pain had gone away. I felt very weak but otherwise normal and I expected that Dr. Owens would tell me I had only suffered from indigestion or something else minor and to resume my trip to New Jersey. So, I was dismayed and frightened when he told me that the only place I was going was to the hospital—and I was to go immediately. He said I wouldn't be allowed to drive so he arranged to have me taken by ambulance to the Mills Hospital located a few blocks from his office.

It didn't take the doctors at Mills Hospital long to determine that I hadn't had a heart attack and while that was good news they weren't able to determine what did cause my chest pain. They were very concerned with my EKG pattern even though Dr. Owens had told them that I had had that pattern for years. I was interned in the Mills Hospital and confined to bed for three days while additional tests were performed and my heart functions were continuously monitored. Ultimately, the doctors at Mills concluded that they had no more tests to prescribe but they believed that my situation was serious. A group of three doctors came into my room and solemnly recommended that I transfer to the Stanford Hospital that had specialized equipment and several world famous cardiac specialists who could perform additional tests. The doctors warned me that some of the tests were risky and there was a 40% chance that I might suffer a serious "event" that included paralysis or death. On the other hand, if my problem wasn't identified, I might drop dead at any moment or suffer some event that would require me to go to an emergency room that wouldn't know how to treat me. I decided to transfer to Stanford and my admittance date was three weeks later. That would give me time to "get my affairs in order" as someone on the hospital staff diplomatically told me.

The warning about the Stanford tests that included the possibility of death caused me to be certain at the deepest level of my being that I actually would die. And I thought it preferable and more convenient for others to die in a hospital rather than to drop dead while driving a car or at home or at work. My belief in the certainty of dying caused me to experience the five stages of grief described eloquently by Dr. Kubler-Ross in her book, *Death and Dying*, i.e., denial, anger, bargaining, depression, and acceptance. Fortunately, I spent very little time in the denial and bargaining stages and rapidly moved from the anger and depression stages to the acceptance stage. I was amazed what a blissful experience the acceptance stage was! I was elated! In fact, more than elated. I had felt this level of bliss before but for only a few moments at a time but during the acceptance stage of my death I was in a blissful stage for several weeks. Some have called this experience a "peak experience" and others a "spiritual awakening" but the best description to me was "unfocused love." While in this state I loved everything about the universe, I accepted my own faults and those of others and accepted normally abhorrent things such as war and disease. Commandments such as "thou shalt not kill" became obvious rules to live by and so obvious that they would be obeyed whether they were written or not. It was natural and easy to be honest. And I experienced a new, more profound way of seeing. In the acceptance stage I could literally see that in addition to looking at a tree *and* grass *and* sky that I could see the objects as one object, that is as tree-grass-sky without using an "and" that created artificial boundaries among objects. When I discovered this new way of seeing, I finally understood that the expression, "at one with the universe," had a factual basis not just a poetic basis. Dick, a wonderful friend and fellow searcher, who also had experienced the bliss of unfocused love, shared with me, "When [in this state] all my questions disappear in a sense of peace and well being at one with the universe where I am at home, no longer a rolling stone." Dick said it well; in one sense there were no questions—there were no problems, but only an "Isness" that the Zen Buddhists spoke of. And I wondered, did the people who we sometimes refer to as gurus or saints obtain their wisdom, their insight, from an unfocused love experience?

I was still in the acceptance stage when I was admitted into the Stanford Hospital and interfaced with Doctor Sheridan. He didn't try to hide his curiosity or puzzlement as he studied my EKG pattern. He told me that at age 34, I was among the youngest ever admitted to the Stanford Hospital "special problems" cardiac ward. I would be a patient for at least a week and my mysterious heart problem combined with my young age made me a curiosity. So in addition to undergoing approved procedures, he forewarned me that a lot of other doctors would want to listen to my heart and some would ask for my permission to perform experimental procedures. His comments were prophetic as not a day passed without a team of doctors entering my room with a permission document for me to sign. Typically, one member of the team would explain the proposed procedure and how it might greatly benefit mankind but on the other hand how it might do great damage to me—it could cause "an event" they euphemistically said. Normally, I would participate in projects that could greatly benefit mankind, but I rejected all their requests. The Stanford doctors confirmed what the doctors at Mills hospital had said. I would undergo some relatively new procedures that had a 40% chance of causing an event that included paralysis or death. If I didn't have the procedures, on the other hand, I might die at any moment. So my situation was already precarious because of the procedures I was scheduled for without subjecting myself to experimental procedures that might cause additional "events." The constant requests to perform experiments on me were annoying but understandable. Stanford was a world-leading research hospital and committed to developing new procedures. Its cardiology department was especially respected because of the presence of Dr. Norman Shumway on their staff, the first United States surgeon to successfully perform a heart transplant.

I was assigned a private room next to a private room occupied by Allen. He had been a cardiac patient with a failing heart in a St. Louis hospital. Their medical staff had concluded that only a heart transplant would save his life but they weren't trained to perform one. He was transferred to the Stanford hospital as a transplant candidate but after a few days of testing, he was told that he didn't meet the qualifications for a new heart. That ended his medical options and as a consequence left him with only a few weeks to live. The first time I passed by his door I was impressed with how pleasing his room had been decorated with banners and flowers and with the happiness on his face as well as on the faces of his visitors. And Allen had visitors most of the time. It may have surprised others that Allen could be so contented since he knew that he was terminal but I understood it. I knew he was in the acceptance stage of dying, just as I was, and he would remain in it for the rest of his short life. During one of the few times when there weren't visitors in his room, I went over, introduced myself and started a conversation. It was one of the most remarkable conversations I ever had. It was so easy and so honest and we talked about anything and everything. Allen and I had impending death in common, so we both thought, and that broke down our defensive barriers immediately. After our conversation, I realized how great life could be if that quality of relationship could happen without requiring something as dramatic as the stimulus of impending death. As a result of my realization, I found my purpose in life that I had been searching for: It was to experience and impart as much unfocused love as possible and not just during dramatic and extraordinary events but during my day-to-day activities.

Even though I had been subjected to over a dozen tests during the week I was in Stanford's cardiac ward, the doctors were unable to find the cause of my heart problem; however, they cautioned me that they still believed I had a serious condition. Fortunately, the high-risk procedures I had been warned about hadn't harmed me at all and my belief that I would die while in the hospital was wrong.

* * * * * *

I never again experienced unfocused love for as long as I did during my heart episode in 1970 but not a day has passed that I haven't had this blissful experience for at least a few minutes and as a result my life changed considerably. Because of the change, I would leave private industry in a few years and pursue a more nurturing career in the academic world.

PART III

CHAPTER **10**

Coda

WHEN MY PHONE rings between midnight and six in the morning, it's always bad news or the wrong number. So I was very apprehensive when I heard it ring and even more so when I picked up the receiver and heard soft crying. It was Mom.

"Your Dad has died," she said, stretching out her words and ending with a sigh of finality.

"I'm sorry. I'm so sorry—but I was afraid of that." I paused to collect my thoughts and then continued, "How did it happen?"

"When I went to bed, he was asleep in that chair of his. Sometime later he yelled out to me. I ran out and asked him what was wrong. He grabbed my hand and said, 'Bless your heart, you're always there.' Then, he passed out and I called an ambulance. But he never did recover. He died shortly after he arrived at the hospital and that was only a couple of hours ago."

"I'm so sorry," I repeated. "I'll be up in Yakima tomorrow afternoon but is there anything I can do right now?"

"No, just get here as fast as you can. We'll have his funeral real soon."

It was about four in the morning on Friday, January 15, 1971 when I received that phone call.

I arrived at my parent's home in Yakima, Washington in mid-afternoon the next day, Saturday. I didn't know what to expect when I rang their doorbell. In the past when I visited them, my ring would cause Mom to yell out to Dad in an excited voice, "He's here!" And then she would swing the door open wide and give me the most wonderful smile combined with a huge hug. This time the only sound was her soft footsteps headed toward the door that she opened slowly. "Son!" she said with a mixture of relief and anguish and then there was a hug that she held for a long time. I was hoping for some inspired words to give her but none came to me. So I walked her to the sofa, sat next to her and held her hand. The large chair that Dad had always sat in was only a few feet away but I didn't feel comfortable looking at it for very long or talking. She was exhausted and was going through the most sorrowful emergency of her life, but Mom found her voice eventually. She told me that she had contacted the Keith and Keith Funeral Home and they'd be taking care of Dad's body and the details of his funeral. The Church of Christ had scheduled a service for him next Monday morning and he would be buried right after the service in the Tahoma Cemetery in Yakima.

I had arrived in Yakima before any of my brothers and sisters. And the one positive thing I had to look forward to while at my parents' home was being with all of them. It would be the first time we would all be together since we lived in Portland, Oregon about twenty-five years previously. But it was not to be—I soon learned from Mom that Joan, who was living in Tampa, was too sick to come to the funeral. But Bill and his wife, Mary, who were living in New Orleans, would arrive on Sunday. J.C.'s home was in San Bernardino, California but he was traveling in Asia on assignment as an Air Force photographer when he received the news about Dad's death. He canceled his Asia assignment and caught a military plane that was flying back to Seattle. From Seattle he would catch a commercial flight and arrive in Yakima late Sunday. My sister Marie had already left her home in Anchorage, Alaska and was scheduled to arrive at the Yakima airport in about two hours. I planned to return to the airport and pick her up. First, though, I persuaded Mom to take a nap until Marie's arrival. She was exhausted, appreciated my suggestion and went to her bedroom.

Thankfully, a couple of neighbors brought us prepared food late Sunday afternoon so we didn't have to be bothered to fix meals for the next few days. At dinnertime on Sunday we sat around the kitchen table very aware that Dad and Joan were not there. Dad's seat at the head of the table was left empty while Mom, now our sole parent, sat at the other end of the table. The atmosphere while understandably gloomy was made worse by travel fatigue that was especially felt by J.C. who had been flying for almost two days non-stop from Asia. We made an attempt to lighten our spirits by talking about our children,

CODA

largely for Mom's benefit who doted on her grandchildren, but seldom saw them. There wasn't a good flow to our talking, though, and we were very tired, so we soon left the table, cleaned up the kitchen and went to bed.

I learned that before the special Monday morning funeral service there would be an open coffin viewing of Dad's body. At first, this alarmed me because it brought back a frightening memory of viewing my dead classmate, Tom, when I was 11 years old and living in Paron, Arkansas. Tom's mouth flew open just as I looked into his coffin. But a friend who worked for a mortician assured me that the reason this happened was because his family had been too poor to embalm him. Fortunately, morticians do know how to prepare a body so there won't be any movement; however, my friend also warned me that the skill of the morticians was so great that they could make the body look too life-like and that could be a shock. I had this warning in mind as our family lined up to look at Dad one last time. Mom, of course, was first in line and per our family custom the rest of us lined up according to age with J.C. right behind Mom, then Marie, then Bill and Mary, and then me. When Mom looked in the coffin, she staggered a bit and yelled, "Oh, no!" J.C. grabbed her, steadied her and walked her to a pew in the front of the church. My friend had been right about the skill of morticians and the consequences. When it was my turn to look into the coffin, I could see that Dad did look very life-like. I was pleased that the mortician had arranged a natural looking smile on his face that he often had when he was sleeping. He was wearing his favorite brown suit, with his favorite tie that he had picked out only a few months before his death. His hands were placed naturally on his body. Since I was the youngest, I was the last one in line for the viewing and the last one to look at Dad before the lid to his coffin was closed forever.

The Church of Christ preacher who conducted Dad's funeral service first announced that Dad had been baptized in the church as a 13-year-old boy, and then he went on to deliver the predictable message that Dad was now in a better place and we should all rejoice in that fact. The preacher actually didn't know anything about him and had never met him. And to my knowledge Dad had never attended his church although he maintained his belief in the unique rightness of the Church of Christ all his life. The rest of the service was essentially biographical in nature and was a bland recitation of Dad's birthplace, age, his professions and the names of his survivors. There were also a few prayers and hymns including, by request from Mom, *The Old Rugged Cross* sung solo by a woman and without musical accompaniment per church beliefs.

It was a large church and that magnified how very few attendees there were. In addition to our immediate family there were only about a half-dozen other people, all volunteers, and none knew our family. This included three men who in addition to my two brothers and me would be the six pallbearers to carry the coffin from the hearse to the gravesite. There were several reasons for such sparse attendance. Dad had been a complex man, didn't make friends easily and generally preferred to be alone rather than associate with other people. He died without having a close friend. Then, too, the frequent moves our family made, averaging more than once a year, made it difficult to maintain even the few relationships that had been started. And not a single member of our extended families was in attendance for the regrettable reason that we didn't know any members outside our immediate family. A case in point, I don't believe Dad even knew the name of his grandparents. Our ignorance was partly the result of family quarrels serious enough that communications had been permanently severed for years. But another major cause of our ignorance was due to a tragedy that occurred in October 1875. Within a few hours of each other, Dad's grandparents died of "milk poisoning" according to some sources or "congestive chills" according to other sources. They left seven infant children, including Dad's father who was just five years old and an estate valued at only $93.27—pitifully small even by 1875 standards. The children became wards of the court and were bound out to different families. A consequence of the family tragedy in 1875 was that no knowledge of family history was passed down. The isolation and loneliness that had origins generations ago rained down on me in 1971 as I sat in the church pew, in part listening to the preacher talking while regretting our meager family connections. It was on that morning of January 18, 1971 that I decided to become a genealogist. I vowed to discover my Good family history as well as the family history of my other three primary ancestral lines and I vowed to make these discoveries within five years—ten at the most. I didn't realize at that time how naïve my goals were and that even after forty years of research the goals would only be partially met.

My feelings of loneliness and thoughts about family history came to an abrupt halt. A loud and final "Amen" from the preacher brought me back to the reality of the funeral. The services inside the Yakima Church of Christ were over. We filed out to the waiting hearse and limousines that would take us to the Tahoma Cemetery.

Funeral processions always got my undivided attention when I saw them and I had seen too many. They made me sad and pensive. I always wondered who the person was in the coffin, what the driver of the hearse was thinking about, and what the family and friends riding in the rest of the procession were thinking about and talking about. Now my perspective was reversed as I sat in the limousine behind the hearse with my family and watched the everyday Yakima automotive and pedestrian traffic pass by. I especially noticed the pedestrians that stopped to stare at our procession and I was touched by and appreciative of one gentleman who removed his hat when he saw our limousine. "He's definitely of the older generation," I thought, "young men don't remove their hat." My thoughts, though, were mostly about Dad and the lonely and complex life he had lived. And it was while riding in his funeral procession, thinking about his life, that I fully realized a vital legacy he had given me—his unwavering commitment to my education through all the many locations we lived. He had arranged for me to finish the fifth and sixth grades in one year and then insisted I go to summer school as a high school student enabling me to finish two grades in one year and graduate when I was only 15. Then, he gave me the encouragement and support to graduate from college when I was only 19. As to what the rest of our family thought about as we rode the three miles to the cemetery, I don't know and I never asked. But I remember very well that we didn't say a word.

The hearse and our limousine parked close to a large tree at the edge of a narrow road through the cemetery and about 30 yards from the open grave that had been prepared for Dad's coffin. The preacher, his wife and another man, who I presumed was an employee of the funeral home, had arrived at the cemetery before us and were standing at the gravesite. We exited the limousine and fortunately all of us had worn warm clothes as it was about forty degrees but made even harder to endure because of a cold breeze. Mom, Marie and Mary were escorted to the gravesite while J.C., Bill and I walked to the back of the hearse where we were met by three men who had been riding in a limousine just behind ours. They were volunteer pallbearers from the church and they introduced themselves and expressed sympathy to my two brothers and me. The introductions were not followed by small talk as some introductions are because we all understood that we would never meet again. The driver of the hearse joined us and opened its back door. He explained that the coffin was sitting on rollers and that he would pull it partially out so we could each grab a handle and carry it to the gravesite with him guiding the way. Then he would direct us how to place the coffin on a temporary platform that was above the open grave. When the six of us lifted the total weight of the coffin, I knew immediately we had a major problem—in fact, a potential disaster! The coffin seemed too heavy for the six of us to carry. I had not even thought about this possibility and it appeared that the funeral home hadn't either. No one had taken the obvious precaution of adding Dad's above average weight to the extra-heavy coffin to see if it was reasonable for six men to carry it. I wondered how my brothers were handling the weight but I couldn't see the expression on their faces because J.C. was the first person on the left side and Bill was the first person on the right side in front of me. I looked across at Jack, the volunteer to my left, however, and I saw panic on his face. I felt the coffin handle I was holding slip a bit in my hand and I felt a tug on my left arm that was so strong that I was afraid my arm would be dislocated from its socket. And then my old nemesis, chest pain, hit me and I thought how ironic it would be to drop dead, as the Stanford doctors had warned me might happen, while carrying my father's coffin. I checked the gravesite to see how much farther we had to carry the coffin and it seemed that we hadn't made any progress at all. I thought of a horror movie I had seen where a man is running to a door to escape but no matter how hard he runs, he doesn't get any closer to the door. Then Jack let out a soft grunt and he shook his head and at the same time my fingers slipped further down the handle I was holding. I decided we would have to gently lower the coffin to the ground and rest briefly rather than face the unacceptable alternative of dropping it. I was about to coordinate with Jack and my brothers to do just that when our guide, the driver of the hearse, said with sensitivity that we greatly appreciated, "OK, now ease Mr. Good onto the platform." We had made it after all. I didn't think we would do it because I didn't think we could do it. But we made it after all.

The number of people at the gravesite was even smaller than the number at the church service and small enough that each of us was very close to the preacher who stood at the gravesite's edge. Ordinarily, I would have been able to hear him very well and to remember what he said because in so many ways it was important. I was not in a good state to listen or to form memories, however. I was just beginning to feel the full impact of Dad's death and I was still stressed from the near catastrophe of dropping his coffin. And my chest pains were still there but now accompanied by atrial fibrillation causing my heart to flop around in my chest. Because of all these distractions I remember only a few of the preacher's words, "The Lord is my Shepherd," and, "Dust to dust," but most of his words were muffled murmurs. I was very relieved when the preacher said "Amen" and he and his wife came to each member of our family, starting with Mom, and expressed their sympathy. We thanked the preacher for providing the services of the church and especially for providing the volunteer pallbearers. The funeral service for Dad had limped to a close.

Over the next 24 hours I used my rental car to drive my siblings and Mary to the Yakima airport for their flights home. Dad's death brought our own mortality into focus and we agreed that it was important to have a family reunion while we were still healthy enough to do it. We promised to make it happen but I noticed that none of us volunteered to coordinate a reunion. Later, I placed a phone call to Joan and summarized the funeral service for her and brought her up to date on all her nieces and nephews. She was enthusiastic about attending a reunion but she didn't volunteer to coordinate one either. I was glad to hear that she was recovering from her illness that prevented her from attending the funeral. But I was alarmed that her doctors had discovered that she, too, had a mysterious heart defect.

My siblings had left Yakima by mid-afternoon the day after the funeral, but I stayed with Mom for another day. I had never spent much time with her alone and so it was a new and pleasant experience just sitting in the living room and reminiscing with her. But as time passed she grew more and more weary and sad. Finally, she got up from her chair without saying anything and went into her bedroom to take a nap, I assumed, but my assumption was wrong. She soon returned and looked totally revitalized and was hugging something against her chest the way little girls hug a stuffed animal. In fact, the expression on her face combined with the way she was hugging reminded me of a little girl. She was holding something that looked like a sack made of very old material, with a lumpy shape, and with pieces of straw sticking out through the material.

"What's that you have there?" I asked.

She gave me a knowing smile and said, "It's my pillow. I took it from my old home in Arkansas. The home I left to marry your father when I was 16."

I was amazed and very surprised because I had never seen it before. It was so surprising because after my siblings left home, when I was 13, it was my job to pack all of Dad and Mom's belongings and put them in our car when we moved. And we got so efficient at moving that I could place all their belongings in the trunk and rear seat of their car. Yet, I had never seen that pillow—so Mom must have hidden it in some of the bedding that she always rolled up when we moved.

"I don't understand. I've never seen it before. Where'd you keep it?"

"I kept it hid all these years from your Dad. Because when he got mad, he sometimes would destroy things and he got real mad at my family—that's why he cut them off and they weren't allowed to visit. I was afraid he'd throw my pillow away. But sometimes when he wasn't around, I'd take it out of hiding and hold it. It gave me lots of comfort."

"It's hard to believe, though, that he didn't know about it considering how long you were married, how little stuff you had, and how often we moved."

"Well, he may have known and just pretended he didn't. When he got mad he got real mad, but he had his kind side too so maybe he knew and just let me have my way. On the other hand, I know how to hide it real good. You didn't know about it did you? And you were the one that loaded up our car!"

"No," I admitted, "I didn't know." Mom seemed so proud of her ability to hide the pillow that I decided I wouldn't ask her where she'd

CODA

hidden it. It would be best for her if she kept her secret, I thought. And I wondered—did Dad come to the same conclusion?

She guessed correctly that I wanted to inspect it so she handed it to me. I could see that the pillow, now water stained, had been made with an "off-beige" material with white and blue flowers and leaves on it. The straw it had been stuffed with had become stiff over time and some had poked through the cover and it looked like quite a bit of straw was missing. Since she had it since she was a girl, and she was born in 1902, I guessed the pillow was made at the turn of the century.

"Did your mother make it?" I asked and handed the pillow back to her.

"Yes. It's the only thing I took with me when I left home except for some clothes." She resumed hugging the pillow and said; "Now, I wonder if there's anything here that you'd like to take back with you—to remember your childhood by."

It was a timely question because I had been thinking about the Bibles and hymnbooks that Dad used to pass out when he held church services and I answered, "How about if I take the hymnbook that has my name in it? Dad offered it to me last year when I was here but it didn't seem right to take it then. Now it does."

Mom thought a long time trying to find the best words and finally answered,

"Your Dad took the books back. Since you didn't take a book last year, he figured it was a sign that he should return all of them to a church like he always said he would."

"What church did he take them to? Was it the Church of Christ where we were yesterday?"

"I don't know but I expect so. All I know is that one of his last trips was to return those books. And when he came back he said, 'I told you I'd return them someday.' "

I said, "Well, that's fine. In fact, I think it's better that he returned them to a church than give them to me."

"He didn't want anyone to think he'd steal let alone steal books from a church. We quarreled a lot about it because I used to think he just plain stole them but he always said he was just borrowing them and would return them one day. In any case, he truly believed that it wasn't stealing if you were helping Jesus and nothing but good would come of it. And you know, looking back on it—he was right. The church he took them from wasn't hurt at all and those books did your Dad and me a lot of good. If you think about it, those books did you a lot of good too."

We had talked for a long time while early evening kept creeping in until our living room was filled with darkness. Mom got out of her chair, still hugging her pillow with one arm, and turned on the living room lights.

NOTES

NOTES

Chapter 2, Making Lye Soap:

I've found that a surprising number of people haven't heard of lye soap and have asked how it was made. Making it does seem somewhat of a lost art but I've described the process below from what I remember about Mom's method combined with information on the Internet.

It takes five ingredients to make lye soap: rendered lard, lye, water, a chicken feather and lots of manual labor.

Rendered lard was made by using fat from a hog's back or from the area around its kidneys (the leaf fat) obtained from a recent hog killing, chopping it into small cubes, heating it in a large container and stirring it frequently until it dissolved. This could be tricky and a bit dangerous because when it got hot, the fat would crackle, pop and small pieces could shoot out of the pan and burn you. After most of the fat had melted, there would initially be some solid pieces of pork on the surface called "cracklings." As the heat continued, all the moisture would be driven from the cracklings and they would then sink to the bottom. At that point, the heat would be removed, and the concoction poured through a cloth to separate the cracklings from the liquid lard. A pound of fat would make about a pint of lard. The cracklings made a tasty, crunchy snack. Mom always kept a bowl full of cracklings whenever she could.

Lye (sodium hydroxide in solution) was made by carefully pouring boiling water into a container partially filled with fine, white hardwood ashes. The liquid solution drained from the bottom of the container might be recycled several times until the solution was strong enough to dissolve a chicken feather. (If a chicken feather wasn't available, it was easy to find someone that could describe another way to test the strength.)

The lye, rendered lard, and additional water was mixed in a large heated cauldron in the back yard and stirred with a long wooden pole. Knowing when to stop stirring was part of the art but Mom said it was when the pole could stand up by itself in the solution. At that point the solution would be poured into molds and allowed to sit for several weeks. The final product was a rugged, yellow bar of lye soap.

Chapter 3, Feeling the Spirit:

Years later I learned that the speaking in tongues experience I witnessed at that Church of God was a well-known phenomena called "glossalalia." Although speaking in tongues is usually associated with Pentecostal Protestant and Charismatic Catholic churches, it is not just a Christian practice and has been witnessed for over a thousand years and in societies as diverse as Eskimo, African, and Haitian. Plato demonstrated that he was well acquainted with glossalalia and there is a record of it as early as 1100 B.C.E. The connection of glossalalia to religion is the belief that some god controls the communication that is fundamentally unintelligible. There is also a related phenomenon, "xenoglossy," where one speaks in a natural language previously unknown to the speaker (some believe this is under god's control.)

Over and above any religious purpose, I believe there were strong social benefits in the experience I witnessed. The congregation was made up of very poor farmers with virtually no entertainment outlets such as movies, radios or newspapers. Dancing and rolling on the floor would be joyful and entertaining experiences. And that rhythm hammered out by the piano served the same purpose as drumming does in some tribal societies—it helps induce a trance. That piano rhythm was as contagious as those in some Rock and Roll music of the 1950s. Jerry Lee Lewis' music especially reminds me of the piano music played in that Church of God.

Another benefit of speaking in tongues is that the speaker can utter virtually anything without any recrimination since it is believed that god is ultimately causing the uttering. I think wives in particular used this opportunity to speak their minds knowing there would be no recriminations from their husbands where ordinarily there would be.

Speaking in tongues enabled the congregation to engage in unfettered, joyful behavior that led to peak experiences and as a bonus strengthened the congregation's social bonds.

Chapter 4, From Segregation to Integration to Segregation:

A military staff oversaw the Arkansas Ordnance Plant (AOP) but it was operated and staffed by civilians. And with so many men serving in the military, aggressive recruiting campaigns were launched to find the large number of workers needed, 14,000 at the peak in November 1942. According to *The Encyclopedia of Arkansas History and Culture*, "---the job of manning the defense plants fell to people that had never been in the labor force before or who had been employed in low-paying work. Handicapped people, women (many who were housewives and had never worked outside the home), young people, older adults, and African Americans were sought for employment. Boys and girls as young as fourteen and fifteen were hired for work." Women, commonly known as WOWs (women ordnance workers), comprised 75% of the work force and African Americans comprised 34%. Consistent with the segregation customs in Arkansas at that time, separate work areas were set aside in the plant for the African American labor force.

Chapter 6, Questions:

1. If the flood that Noah endured were caused by 40 days and 40 nights of rain, what would be the required average rainfall to cover the entire earth? The floodwaters would have to cover Mt. Everest whose altitude is approximately 5.5 miles above sea lever. The required rainfall is approximately 6 inches per minute all over the planet. The present world record for rainfall of 0.06 inches per minute established in 1966 on Reunion Island, not far from Madagascar, is a factor of 100 less than that required.

2. Where did the water come from to flood the entire earth? The hydrosphere, that is the total amount of water in the earth as well as the atmosphere, has a volume of about 329 million cubic miles. The water needed for the flood is about one billion cubic miles leaving a shortage of over 600 million cubic miles. Of course, if a god exists like the one in the Noah's Ark legend, that god wouldn't have to comply with the laws of science as mere mortals have to.

That god could create any amount of water needed from anything, including from nothing. Did a god do that?

Chapter 10, Coda:

Mom died in Yakima, Washington on February 23, 1978. She was buried in the Tahoma Cemetery located in Yakima and she shares a joint headstone with Dad with the inscription, *Together Forever.*

After her death, the pillow she had kept hidden since her marriage in 1918 was given to me and I, in turn, have given it to my daughter Marian.